SECRETS REVEALED

CLAIRVOYANCE, MAGIC AND THE REALITY OF SPIRITS

C. W. Leadbeater

THE BOOK TREE
San Diego, California

First published 1911
as part of *Gems of Thought*
Progressive Thinker Publishing
Chicago, IL

© 1911 M.E. Cadwallader
New material including title, revisions and cover
© 2003
The Book Tree
All rights reserved

ISBN 1-58509-217-7

Cover layout & design
Lee Berube

Printed on Acid-Free Paper
in the United States of America

Published by
The Book Tree
P O Box 16476
San Diego, CA 92176
www.thebooktree.com

We provide fascinating and educational products to help awaken the public to new ideas and information that would not be available otherwise.
Call 1 (800) 700-8733 for our *FREE BOOK TREE CATALOG*.

INTRODUCTION

What follows is a rare collection of lectures by C.W. Leadbeater never before published in a volume by itself. Leadbeater was an extremely prolific and respected writer on psychic development and was once a spiritual teacher at the renowned Theosophical Society. This work is one of the most important and revealing that he has ever done. That is why we titled it *Secrets Revealed*—because he shares so many in-depth secrets that are not found or revealed elsewhere.

C.W. Leadbeater

The first part of the book is devoted entirely to clairvoyance and psychic powers. It begins with a section called Clairvoyance in Space, which covers five different ways it is experienced while being far from events. He tells some amazing real-life stories of clairvoyance in action, which leaves little doubt that such things are real.

The next section, Clairvoyance in Time, shows how it is possible to see events from the past or future. One area of interest here is psychometry, where a sensitive person can take a physical object and tell its history, where it was located and what events may have taken place around it. A number of maverick archaeologists are currently using these methods. Leadbeater gives a great example of this happening after he handed a tiny fragment of stone from Stonehenge to a skilled women in the art.

The section after this is called How to Develop Clairvoyance. Here we learn what it takes to become good at it, plus helpful tips are included on what not to do as well. It is brilliant advice coming from a skilled and gifted master. He covers concentration, moral development, meditation and more.

Once one is skilled in clairvoyance it is time for the next part, called Use and Abuse of Psychic Powers. He makes clear the difference between one who receives training in this area and one who does not. He highly recommends the former, as proper and respectful use of these skills will most always result from proper training. The best teachers, according to Leadbeater, are in India. One important aspect in using such powers is to avoid personal gain and focus instead on the common good. His teachings, however, go far beyond this basic premise.

The second half of the book jumps into other subjects. The first is Magic, White and Black. He explains the difference between each, then covers angels, elementals, nature spirits, talismans, evocation and provides some simple safeguards against evil.

Leadbeater closes the book with The Rationale of Apparitions. This is an incredible collection of ghost stories. He states that anyone, expert or non-expert, who has ever put any attention into the subject knows that they exist. With serious research it becomes impossible to deny. Leadbeater shares some of that research here—including stories of human spirits who have returned for help, and also to provide help to others.

This is an extremely rich collection of material. Those who have spent years delving into these subjects may still wonder why they have never seen or heard of this information before.

Paul Tice

CONTENTS

1. Clairvoyance in Space   1
2. Clairvoyance in Time   13
3. How to Develop Clairvoyance   27
4. Use and Abuse of Psychic Powers   45
5. Magic, White and Black   67
6. The Rationale of Apparitions   93

Clairvoyance in Space.

A Lecture Delivered Before a Chicago Audience, by C. W. Leadbeater, the Great Psychic, of London, England.

VARIETIES OF CLAIRVOYANCE—MAGICAL AND GENUINE CLAIRVOYANCE—ILLUSTRATION BY WIRELESS TELEGRAPHY — THOUGHT-FORM CLAIRVOYANCE—TRANCE AND ASTRAL VISIT—USING THE MENTAL BODY—CRYSTAL GAZING—INTERESTING PSYCHIC INCIDENTS—MEANINGLESS VISIONS.

We spoke last week of what a man would see with opened sight if he simply looked round him just where he stood, without making any effort to penetrate into the distance, either of space or time. To-day we have to consider the capacity to see events or scenes removed from the seer in space and too far distant for ordinary observation. When a man in one continent observes and reports what is taking place in another, thousands of miles away, how is it done?

VARIETIES OF CLAIRVOYANCE.

Some people may think that the first question ought to be, is it ever done? Yes, there is no doubt whatever that it has been done very often. Anyone who is as yet uncertain as to this should read the large numbers of authenticated instances given in the literature of the subject. Cases will be found in the reports of the Psychical Research Society, and in almost any account of Spiritualistic phenomena. There can be no question in the minds of those who have studied the subject that clairvoyance in space is a possibility—indeed, for us in Theosophy this is so definitely so that we know no less than five ways in which it can be done, as I shall proceed to explain. Of these five ways, four are really varieties of clairvoyance, while the fifth does not properly come under that head at all, but belongs to the domain of magic. I mention it here only because a person who was endeavoring to classify cases of clairvoyance would sooner or later come across cases of its use, and would very likely be puzzled by them. People often write to Theosophists and describe some experience connected with non-physical life, and ask how the result was produced, and sometimes such questions are very difficult to answer—not because the phenomena are rare, but because they are so common; not that there is any difficulty in accounting for them, but that there are so many ways in which they might have occurred, that without full and careful cross-examination it is impossible to say which method was actually employed.

MAGICAL AND GENUINE CLAIRVOYANCE.

But one may usually distinguish this magical procedure from genuine clairvoyance, because its leading feature is that it is not by any faculty of the seer that information is obtained; in fact, he does not see what happens at all, but he is told by another. He simply sends somebody to see from him, though when he has learnt what he wishes to know, he very likely gives it out as though he had seen it himself. In the East this method is largely employed, and the messenger there is usually a nature-spirit, whose assistance may be obtained either by invocation or by evocation; that is to say, the operator may either persuade his astral coadjutor by prayers and offerings to give him such help as he desires, or he may compel his aid by the determined exercise of a highly developed will and certain magical ceremonies. The same thing is often done at a Spiritualistic seance, but there the messenger employed is more likely to be a dead man, though sometimes there, too, it is only an obliging nature-spirit, who is amusing himself by posing as somebody's departed relation. Of course there are also cases in which the medium is a clairvoyant, but much more often some dead man goes and sees what is needed, and then comes back and describes it through the organism of the medium. Whichever be the method or the messenger, we may dismiss as not genuine clairvoyance any case in which the faculty employed is not that of the seer himself.

One who possesses the type of clairvoyance of which we spoke last week, and is able to see the astral entities as they move about him, is not therefore necessarily also dowered with this faculty of seeing at a distance. He would still have to learn this, though it ought not to be difficult for him to acquire it, and it would be done by one of the four methods which I shall try to describe.

The first has certain analogies on the physical plane, but none of them are perfect. If you can imagine a telephone along the wire of which we could see instead of hearing, that would give a partial analogy. Think of the new system of wireless telegraphy; the vibrations spread out in all directions, but suppose they spread in one direction only, and made a kind of temporary wire as they moved by arranging or magnetizing or polarizing the particles of the ether so that for the time a special current could pass along them, then we should have another analogy; and by combining the two ideas we shall have a fair image of this kind of clairvoyance, which has sometimes been called seeing by means of an astral current. By an effort of will such action may be set up among astral particles as to form a line of them along which the clairvoyant may see, something as though he were looking through a telescope. This method has the disadvantage that this telegraph line or telescope is liable to disarrangement or even destruction by any sufficiently strong astral current which happens to cross its path; but if the original effort of will were fairly definite, this would not often happen. The view of distant events obtained in this way is usually not unlike that gained by means of a telescope. Figures appear very small, like those upon a distant stage, and they are often seen in the midst of a disc of light, as though they were scenes thrown upon a sheet from a magic lantern. The observer has no power to shift his point of view so as to understand better what he sees, nor can he, as a rule, exercise any further faculty; he would not, for example, be able to hear what was being said among those distant actors.

In this case the consciousness of the clairvoyant remains at this end of the line, so that he is able to use his physical organs while he sees, and can describe everything as it occurs. This is one of the commonest orders of sight at a distance, and for many people it is very much facilitated if they have some physical object which can be used as a starting-point for their astral telegraph line or tube—a convenient focus for their will-power. A ball of crystal is the commonest and most effectual of such aids, since it has the advantage of possessing within itself qualities which stimulate psychic faculty. There are plenty of cases on record in which by means of a crystal men have seen what took place at a distance; but this belongs more properly to a later stage of our subject.

THOUGHT-FORM CLAIRVOYANCE.

Let us compare this with another type of clairvoyance—that by means of a thought-form. All students of Theosophy are aware that thought takes form on its own plane, and very much of it upon the astral plane as well; and in some cases this thought takes the form of the thinker. If a man thinks of himself very strongly as present at a certain place or wishes very strongly to be there, he will often project an image of himself which will be visible to clairvoyant sight. Normally the man has no control over such a form when it has once left him, but there are methods by which a man may retain such connection with it as may enable him to receive impressions through it—to use it as a kind of outpost of his consciousness. In such cases, the impressions made upon the form would be conveyed to the seer not along a line of astral particles, as in the last case, but by sympathetic vibration. In exercising this type of sight, the operator will still be perfectly conscious at his own end of the line, and so can describe as he sees, so long as he does not allow the intentness of his thought to be disturbed. If he loses that for an instant, the whole vision vanishes. But he had advantages over the man using the astral current, in that he sees his figures life-size, as though he were close to them, and may also to some extent shift his point of view if he wishes. Instances of this kind of sight among untrained people are naturally rarer than the other, since it requires greater mental control.

TRANCE, AND ASTRAL VISIT.

There is, however, another and still more efficient variety of this sight, which would present somewhat different symptoms to the observer. If your seer fell into a trance, so that his physical consciousness was for the time unavailable, and it was only after his return that he could describe what he had seen—then you have probably an example of this other type of clairvoyance in which the information is gained by an astral visit. Instead of seeing from a distance or sending a messenger, the man simply goes and sees for himself, which is in many ways much the most satisfactory way. In this case he will describe himself as standing among the actors in his scene, hearing what they say as well as seeing what they do, able to move about freely as he wishes. Manifestly this is a greater achievement and altogether a more efficient faculty, for the man who possesses it fully can see and study at leisure all the other inhabitants of the astral plane, so that the great world of nature-spirits lies open before him, and he may converse at will with them, and even with some of the lower devas or angels. Wherever he goes, he goes in full consciousness, with full power of investigation. True, it has its own special dangers for the untrained seer, and they are greater than those of either of the other methods; yet it is the most satisfactory form of clairvoyance open to him, for the immensely superior variety which we shall next consider is not available except for specially trained students.

This last method, which is so much the best and highest, consists simply of using the mental body instead of the astral vehicle, which naturally requires much greater development. In this body the man travels just as in the other case, but without any of the dangers which beset the path of the astral visitor, and with the enormous advantages which the possession of the higher faculties of the mental plane gives in the way of additional sight and wider knowledge. In his travels he sees so much more and has so much greater opportunities chiefly because he has the capacity of entering upon all the glory and beauty of the higher land of bliss, so that for him heaven is always open, not as a faraway vision, but as an ever-present reality in which he is living and moving at will.

We see, therefore, that, besides the magical method first mentioned, we have four types of clairvoyance—that by an astral telescope, that dependent upon the projection of a thought-form, that involving an astral visit, and that which needs the use of the mental body. The man who possesses either of these latter has obviously many and great advantages at his disposal, even besides those already enumerated. Not only can he visit without trouble or expense all the beautiful and famous places of the earth, but if he happens to be a scholar, think what it must mean to him that he has access to all the libraries of the world! What must it be for the scientifically-minded man to see taking place before his eyes so many of the processes of the secret chemistry of nature, or for the philosopher to have revealed to him so much more than ever before of the working of the great mysteries of life and death. To him those who are gone from this plane are dead no longer, but living and within reach for a long time to come; for him many of the conceptions of religion are no longer matters of faith, but of knowledge. Above all, he can join the army of invisible helpers, and really be of use on a large scale. Certainly it has its dangers also, especially for the untrained; dangers from evil entities of various kinds, which may terrify or injure those who allow themselves to lose the courage to face them boldly; danger of deception of all sorts, of misconceiving and misinterpreting what is seen; greatest of all, the danger of becoming conceited about the thing and of thinking it impossible to make a mistake. But a little common-sense and a little experience should protect a man against these.

It must not be forgotten that the man who acquires these powers under the guidance of a qualified teacher will be bound by certain restrictions. Briefly, these will be that there shall be no prying, no selfish use of the power, and no displaying of phenomena. That is to say, the same considerations of honor and good feeling which would govern the actions of a gentleman upon this plane are expected to apply upon the astral and mental planes also; that the pupil is never under any circumstances to use the power which his additional knowledge gives him in order to promote his own worldly advantage, or indeed in connection with gain in any way, and never to give what is called in Spiritualistic circles "a test"—that is, to do anything which will incontestably prove to skeptics on the physical plane that he possesses what to them would appear to be an abnormal power. With regard to this latter proviso people often say "Why should he not? It would be so easy to convince and confute the skeptic, and it would do him good!" Such critics lose sight of the fact that, in the first place, none of those who know anything want to confute or convince skeptics, or indeed ever trouble themselves about the skeptic's attitude in the slightest degree one way or the other; and in the second, they fail to understand how much better it is for that skeptic that he should gradually grow into an intellectual appreciation of the facts of nature, instead of being suddenly introduced to them by a knock-down blow, as it were.

CRYSTAL GAZING, ETC.

So far we have been considering what these powers would be to him who possessed them fully, and had been trained to use them. But the majority of cases with which an investigator of the subject would come into contact would naturally fall very far short of these. He may meet with a few instances of intentional clairvoyance, when the seer definitely sets himself to discover a certain fact, and succeeds to a greater or less extent. But he will find far more who see unintentionally and spasmodically without any idea beforehand when the faculty will manifest itself. Another class, standing between these two, is that of those who intentionally put themselves in the way of seeing something, but do not in the least know what it will be, nor have any control over the sight when the visions have begun. They may be said to be psychic Micawbers, who put themselves into a receptive condition, and simply wait for something to turn up. The commonest variety of these is the crystal-gazer. Sometimes, but comparatively rarely, he is able to direct his vision in his crystal as he wishes; but the majority of such gazers just form a fortuitous astral tube and see whatever happens to present itself at the end of it. The crystal is for them simply a focus from which their clairvoyant line starts, and is not really a necessity at all, though they usually think that they could not do anything without it.

Any sort of polished surface may be employed. I have heard of a mirror being used, or a glass ball, or a bottle of water, and it may be recollected that Lane describes the use of ink for this purpose in his introduction to the "Arabian Nights." A drop of blood is used among the Maoris in New Zealand, and I have even heard of a saucer of charcoal being employed. Mr. Andrew Lang in his "Dreams and Ghosts" gives us a very good example of the purposeless kind of vision most frequently seen in this way. He says: "I had given a glass ball to a young lady, Miss Baillie, who had scarcely any success with it. She loaned it to Miss Leslie, who saw a large square old-fashioned red sofa covered with muslin, which she found in the next country-house she visited. Miss Baillie's brother, a young athlete, laughed at these experiments, took the ball into the study, and came back looking 'gey gash.' He admitted that he had seen a vision—somebody he knew, under a lamp. He would discover during the week whether he saw right or not. This was at 5:30 on a Sunday afternoon.

"On Tuesday Mr. Baillie was at a dance in a town some forty miles from his home, and met a Miss Preston. 'On Sunday,' he said, 'about half-past five you were sitting under a standard lamp in a dress I never saw you wear, a blue blouse with lace over the shoulders, pouring out tea for a man in blue serge, whose back was towards me, so that I only saw the tip of his moustache.' 'Why, the blinds must have been up!' said Miss Preston. 'I was at Dulby,' said Mr. Baillie, and he undeniably was."

This is quite a typical case of crystal-gazing—the picture correct in every detail, you see, and yet absolutely unimportant and bearing no apparent signification of any sort to either party, except that it served to prove to Mr. Baillie that there was something in crystal-gazing. But it is sometimes exactly in this apparently aimless, accidental sort of way that the first gleam of a higher vision comes to a person. Sometimes it is because the physical body is temporarily weakened by illness, so that for the moment its insistent faculties are not so much in evidence, and so the others which are usually hidden are able to show through. Sometimes it is an effort from the outside which for a moment makes a person sensitive to what normally would not be able to impress him. We have a very good example of this in Dr. Bushnell's work, "Nature and the Supernatural."

The story runs that a certain Captain Yonnt had a twice-repeated dream, in which he very clearly saw a party of emigrants perishing from cold and hunger at a spot in the mountains, the scenery of which was strongly impressed upon his mind. On describing it in the morning to an old hunter, the latter recognized the scenery at once; and this fact so profoundly impressed Captain Yonnt that he forthwith set off to find the place, being persuaded that the emigrants were really there, according to his dream. All proved to be exactly as he had seen it, and he was enabled to save the lives of the people. It would seem probable that some helper, observing the forlorn condition of the emigrant party, took the nearest impressible and otherwise suitable person (who happened to be the Captain) to the spot in the astral body, and

CLAIRVOYANCE IN SPACE.

aroused him sufficiently to fix the scene firmly in his memory.

Sometimes when two people are in very close sympathy, we find that a bond exists between them which enables one of them to impress the other in this way at some great crisis or in some serious need. I remember a case told in the proceedings of the Society for Psychical Research about an English general who was seriously wounded in one of the battles in the Indian mutiny, and supposed himself to be dying. As he was being borne off the field, he said to one of the officers near him, "Take this ring off my finger, and send it to my wife," and the officers promised him to do so. His wife at this particular moment had just lain down in bed, but was still wide awake when she saw the whole scene as in a vision, and heard her husband make the request above described. It was only some days later that she learnt that her husband had really been seriously wounded at the assault upon Mooltan, and that he had actually made the request about the ring as she seemed to hear it in the vision. In this instance obviously it was the intimate sympathy between husband and wife which made the rapport possible, and then the general's earnest thought of his wife acting upon a mind already so closely attuned to his conveyed the picture to her, so that she saw and heard practically as though she had been present in the flesh. Probably he may have definitely wished that she were with him, or at any rate that he could see her before his death. So strong a thought as this does not, however, seem to be indispensable, for there are cases in which clairvoyance has been produced, and the necessary link supplied, by a thought which was not at all of that nature, and not even apparently connected with any definite wish. A case illustrating this is to be found in the proceedings of the Psychical Research Society, Vol. II, p. 160:

"Mrs. Broughton awoke one night in 1844 and roused her husband, telling him that something dreadful had happened in France. He begged her to go to sleep again, and not trouble him. She assured him that she was not asleep when she saw what she insisted on telling him. First, a carriage accident—which she did not actually see, but what she saw was the result—a broken carriage, a crowd collected, a figure gently raised and carried into the nearest house, then a figure lying on a bed, which she then recognized as the Duke of Orleans. Gradually friends collecting round the bed, among them several members of the French royal family; the queen, then the king, all silently and tearfully watching the evidently dying duke. One man (she could see his back, but did not know who he was) was a doctor. He stood bending over the duke, feeling his pulse, with his watch in the other hand. And then all passed away, and she saw no more. As soon as it was daylight she wrote down in her journal all that she had seen. It was before the days of the electric telegraph, and two or more days passed before the papers announced the death of the Duke of Orleans. Visiting Paris a short time afterwards, she saw and recognized the place of the accident and received the explanation of her impression. The doctor who attended the dying duke was an old friend of hers, and as he watched by the bed his mind had been constantly occupied with her and her family."

Evidently in this case the link was formed by the doctor's frequent thought about Mrs. Broughton, yet he clearly had no especial wish that she should see what he was doing at the time. Evidently also, the clairvoyance was of the "astral telescope" type, as is shown by the fixity of her point of view —which, be it observed, was not the doctor's point of view sympathetically transferred (as it might easily have been) since she sees his back without recognizing him.

MEANINGLESS VISIONS.

There is a large class of clairvoyant visions which have no traceable cause, which are apparently quite meaningless, and have no recognizable relation to any events known to the seer. To this class belong many of the landscapes seen by some people just before they fall asleep. The scenes appear to be selected entirely at haphazard, just as though one seized a physical telescope and turned it vaguely upon the landscape without looking first to see at what it was pointed. Sometimes what are seen are not landscapes but faces, or clouds of color. One of the best descriptions of this sort of scene that I know is given by Mr. W. T. Stead in his "Real Ghost Stories," p. 65:

"I got into bed, but was not able to sleep. I shut my eyes and waited for sleep to come; instead of sleep, however, there came to me a succession of curiously vivid clairvoyant pictures. There was no light in the room and it was perfectly dark; I had my eyes shut also. But notwithstanding the darkness I suddenly was conscious of looking at a scene of singular beauty. It was as if I saw a living miniature about the size of a magic-lantern slide. At this moment I can recall the scene as if I saw it again. It was a seaside piece. The moon was shining upon the water, which rippled slowly on to the beach. Right before me a long mole ran out into the water. On either side of the mole irregular rocks stood up above the sea-level. On the shore stood several houses, square and rude, which resembled nothing that I had ever seen in house architecture. No one was stirring, but the moon was there and the sea and the gleam of the moonlight on the rippling waters, just as if I had been looking on the actual scene.... I was wide awake, and at the same time that I saw the scene I distinctly heard the dropping of the rain outside the window. Then suddenly, without any apparent object or reason, the scene changed. The moonlit sea vanished, and in its place I was looking right into the interior of a reading-room. It seemed as if it had been used as a schoolroom in the daytime, and was employed as a reading-room in the evening. I remember seeing one reader hold up a magazine or book in his hand and laugh. It was not a picture— it was there. The scene was just as if you were looking through an opera-glass; you saw the play of the muscles, the gleaming of the eye, every movement of the unknown persons in the unnamed place into which you were gazing. I saw all that without opening my eyes, nor did my eyes have anything to do with it. You see such things as these as it were with another sense which is more inside your head than in your eyes. This was a very poor and paltry experience, but it enabled me to understand better how it is that clairvoyants see than any amount of disquisition. The pictures were apropos of nothing; they had been suggested by nothing I had been reading or talking of; they simply came as if I had been able to look through a glass at what was occurring somewhere else in the world. I had my peep, and then it passed, nor have I had a recurrence of a similar experience."

This seems as absolutely casual as the glimpse one gets through a gap in the hedge when one is driving along a road; yet it had its value for Mr. Stead, for it gave him that one touch of personal experience which is worth so much to the investigator. How this direct evidence may be systematically obtained will be the subject of our fourth lecture on Clairvoyance; but short of undertaking the personal development which will give us first-hand experience, very much may be learnt from the literature of the subject. I have myself presented the Theosophical theory of clairvoyance in a treatise on the matter, an epitome of which I am giving in these lectures. To that book I would refer those who wish for further detail, as they will find in it all that I have now said, and much more. From it also they may get the names of other books in which collections of illustrations can be found; and in this way they may study the subject through the eyes of those who have investigated it, and may acquire some idea of the great mass of evidence that lies within their reach.

In describing to you to-night these various kinds of clairvoyance I have mentioned nothing of which I have not myself seen instances; and what I have seen you may see, if you are willing to take the trouble which I took. There is no mystery as to the methods either of investigation or of self-development; they are fully and clearly described in the Theosophical literature, and all that is necessary is the resolution to make the effort. Few things, surely, can be more interesting than a study which opens up to us so wide a field, which gives us so far grander and truer a conception of this beautiful world in which the Divine Power has placed us in order that through the lessons to be learnt here we may qualify ourselves for the glorious future which He has destined for us all.

Clairvoyance in Time.

A Lecture Delivered Before a Chicago Audience, by
C. W. Leadbeater, the Great Psychic,
of London, England.

VISIONS OF THE REMOTE PAST—THE CONSCIOUSNESS OF THE LOGOS—DIFFICULTY OF EXPRESSING RECORDS—PSYCHOMETRIC DELINEATIONS—FORESEEING WHAT HAS NOT HAPPENED—TWO METHODS OF PREVISION—ANOTHER KIND OF PREVISION.

We examined last week the question of clairvoyance in space, and considered the various ways in which it is possible for a man to see what is taking place at a distance. Tonight we have another problem—that of trying to understand how it is possible for a man to see what happened long ago in the past, or what will happen in the future. In this case I may again repeat what I said last week, that there is no question at all that this can be done, and has been done times without number. The authenticated cases of what is called "second sight" among the Highlanders of Scotland are in themselves quite sufficient to furnish evidence to convince the most skeptical. Once more, as with mesmerism, with apparitions, with Spiritualism, I am not speaking for those who are still ignorant of the facts of the case and therefore do not yet know that these things happen, but for those who wish to know how they are done. Those who are unfamiliar with the facts should study the literature of the subject, which is a very considerable one.

VISIONS OF THE REMOTE PAST.

Let us divide our subject into two parts which naturally

occur as one thinks of it, and take up separately the power of looking back and the power of looking forward. We shall find that both these powers are possessed by different people in very varying degrees, ranging from the man who has both faculties fully at his command, down to one who only occasionally gets involuntary and very imperfect glimpses or reflections of the scenes of other days. Take first the case of a detailed vision of the remote past; how is it possible that this can be obtained? Broadly speaking, it is possible because there is such a thing as memory of Nature—a record of every occurrence made automatically as it takes place. Nothing can happen that does not indelibly impress itself, and the record which it leaves can be read forever after by the man who learns how this is done. Where and how is the impression made, you will say? In order to understand something of that, we shall have to try to carry our thoughts very high indeed, for we must raise them towards the consciousness of Him who made the system, and make an effort to image to ourselves how its events will be likely to present themselves to Him. His mind is far above our imperfect comprehension, yet we can reason upwards towards it to a certain limited extent. It is found, as I have said before, that it is possible for man to develop within himself the consciousness of higher levels, and though of course the highest of these is infinitely below the Divine consciousness, yet it is obvious that it must at least be nearer to it than the entirely undeveloped consciousness. So that if we note the line along which this exalted consciousness differs from that of the physical plane, we shall at least be looking upward toward the Divine; and by carrying on the same idea to the utmost limit of our mental capacity we shall form a conception of His consciousness which will be not inaccurate as far as it goes, though naturally hopelessly inadequate. Whatever we can imagine along that line of development, all that, and infinitely more, He must be. All religions tell us that the Deity is omnipresent; in our Theosophical study we reach the very same conclusion, though by quite a different line.

Those who have examined the illustrations of the higher bodies of man which I have given in my new book on the subject will recollect that, as the man develops, his vehicles not only improve in color and luminosity, but also grow in size. The aura, the luminous colored mist surrounding the physical body of man, may be seen by clairvoyant sight at various levels, because it contains matter of different degrees of density, so that whether a man be using the sight of his astral body, his mental body, or even his causal body, there will be something in it for him to see. But all the experience gained through these lower vehicles is all the while being stored up by the man himself, who is thereby steadily developing qualities and increasing his consciousness; he is, as it were, a reservoir of force, and more and more energy is being stored up within him. To retain this, and to give it due expression, he eventually needs a larger causal body, and so it comes that the highly-evolved man, as seen by the clairvoyant, is readily recognizable by this feature as well as by increasing splendor in light and color. This is by no means a new idea to students of these matters, for it may be found in the Oriental books. It is stated in Buddhist literature that the aura of the Buddha had a very unusual extension, and that its influence might be felt at a great distance from his physical body. We know that if we come into the presence of a strongly magnetic person we at once feel his influence, and this is in reality nothing but the vibration sent out from his higher vehicles. There are some people with whom we dislike to come into close contact, and others to whom we feel it a blessing to be near, and this again is because we sense their vibrations, though often without knowing it. In the case of the evolved man, we absolutely enter his aura when we approach his bodily presence, and so we are strongly influenced and brought for the time into harmony with his vibrations. We have only to extend this idea to understand how a great Adept may shower blessing upon a whole neighborhood merely by his presence, and how a still greater one may include the entire world itself within his aura; and from this we may gradually lead our minds up to the conception that there is a Being so exalted as to comprehend within Himself the whole of our solar system. And we should remember that, enormous as this seems to us, it is but as the tiniest drop in the vast ocean of space.

So of the Logos (who has in Him all the capacities and qualities with which we can possibly endow the highest God we can imagine) it is literally true, as was said of old, that "of Him and through Him and to Him are all things," and "in Him we live and move and have our being." I was once told in India by a Muhammadan scholar that this was the true meaning of the daily cry of the muezzin from his minaret, as he calls the faithful to prayer—"La illah il allah," which is commonly translated, "There is no God but God." The statement made by this learned man was that the true translation should be rather, "There is nothing but God"; and if that be so, we have here a very beautiful expression from an unexpected quarter of the eternal truth that all His system is a manifestation of Him, and that in all its worlds there can be nothing that is not He.

THE CONSCIOUSNESS OF THE LOGOS.

Now if this be so, it is clear that whatever happens within our system happens absolutely within the consciousness of its Logos, and so we at once see that the true record must be its memory. Furthermore, it is obvious that, on whatever plane that wondrous memory exists, it cannot but be far above anything that we know; consequently, whatever records we may find ourselves able to read must be only a reflection of that great dominant fact, mirrored in the denser media of the lower planes On the astral plane it is at once evident that this is so—that what we are dealing with is only a reflection of a reflection, and an exceedingly imperfect one, for such records as can be reached there are fragmentary in the extreme, and often seriously distorted. The medieval alchemists often employed water as a symbol of astral matter, and it certainly is a remarkably apt one. From the surface of still water we may get a clear reflection of the surrounding objects, just as from a mirror; but at the best it is only a two-dimensional representation of three-dimensional things, and therefore it differs in all its qualities, except color, from that which it represents and is always reversed as well.

But suppose the surface of the water is ruffled by the wind, what do we find then? A reflection still, certainly, but so broken up and distorted as to be quite useless or even misleading as a guide to the shape and real appearance of the objects reflected. Here and there for a moment we might happen to get a clear picture of some tiny part of the scene —of a single leaf from a tree, for example; but it would need long labor and considerable knowledge of natural laws to build up anything like a true conception of the whole obect by putting together even a large number of such isolated fragments of an image of it.

Perhaps such reffections are more often seen than people realize, for much that is taken for meaningless vision or dream is actually a glimpse of a record of the past. But the untrained clairvoyant can do but little with such a glimpse even when he gets it; he is usually quite unable to relate it to what occurred before or after it, or to account for anything extraordinary which may appear in it. The trained man who sees a higher reflection on the mental plane is able to deal very differently with his picture; he can follow the drama connected with it backwards or forwards to any extent that may seem desirable, and can trace out with equal ease the causes which led up to it or the results which it in its turn will produce. The record there is full and accurate, and cannot be mistaken. Even there there is still a difference between different observers—not that it would be possible at that level to see wrongly, but that a certain personal equation enters into the transference of the memory to this physical plane. Our observations in this world have precisely similar limitations. If a dozen people look at the same scene together, no two of them will give exactly the same description of it afterwards. Each will seize upon what interests him the most; the botanist will describe the trees and plants very fully, the geologist will scarcely notice the trees, but will carefully note the type of the soil and the age of the rocks; the farmer will note the quality of the soil from another point of view, while the artist will ignore all these points, but will have a keen eye for bits of color or for beauties of form, and will probably bring away a better grasp of the scene as a whole than any of the others.

DIFFICULTY IN EXPRESSING RECORDS.

In exactly the same way, though many observers may see simultaneously the same record on the mental plane, their accounts of it on the physical plane may sometimes be disproportionate, each attaching most importance to what appeals most to him individually. It is in the nature of things impossible that any account given down here of a vision or experience on the mental plane can be complete, since nine-tenths of what is seen and felt there cannot be expressed by physical words at all; and since all expression must therefore be partial, there is obviously some possibility of selection as to the part expressed. Still, allowing for these slight and unaccountable divergences, we find in practice that accounts from the mental plane agree, and so by long-continued experiment and verification we learn that we can depend upon the records at this level as correct. There still remains, however, the impossibility of fully expressing them in words. The difficulty is analogous to that which a painter finds in putting before us a landscape. The most perfect picture is simply a very ingenious attempt to make upon only one of our five senses, by means of lines and colors on a flat surface, an impression similar to that which would have been made if we had actually had before us the scene depicted. The picture itself really shows us but little, and it is the brain which from its previous experience supplies what is missing. Thus if we show a picture to a savage or to an animal, in many cases he is quite unable to understand what it means. If he has no previous experience, if he has never seen anything resembling the subject of the picture, it suggests but little to him.

The clairvoyant labors under just such difficulties, but to a far greater degree, in his efforts to describe in the terms of a three-dimensional world the facts of one which is built on a wider plan—which has an extension in a direction incomprehensible to the physical brain. If you try to study along the lines of the fourth dimension you will understand what I mean, and you will see how from that point of view the limitations which we call time and space are so much modified that they have practically ceased to exist. It is evident from the study of the highest consciousness in man, that in the Divine consciousness this record must be something very much more than memory; for clearly to Him the past, present and future cannot hold at all the same relation as they do to our sight; they must all exist side by side, they must be simultaneously present.

Thirty years ago I met with a very curious little book which tried to explain this scientifically from the orthodox religious point of view. Its arguments were so ingenious that I should like to reproduce the outline of them for you. It began by the undeniable statement that we see everything by light either emitted or reflected by it, and that that light travels through space at a certain recognized rate—186,000 miles per second. As far as anything in our own world is concerned, this may be considered as practically instantaneous, but when we come to deal with interplanetary distances we have to take the speed of light into account. For example, it takes eight minutes and a quarter for it to travel to us from the sun, so that when we look at the solar orb we see it by means of a ray of light which left it more than eight minutes ago.

From this follows a very curious result. The ray of light by which we see the sun can obviously report to us only the state of affairs which existed in that luminary when it started on its journey, and would not be in the least affected by anything that happened there after it left; so that we really see the sun not as he is, but as he was eight minutes ago. That is to say that if anything of importance took place in the sun, such as the formation of a new sun-spot, an astronomer who is watching the orb through his telescope at the time would be quite unaware of the incident while it was happening, since the ray of light bearing the news would not reach him until more than eight minutes later. The difference is more striking when we consider the fixed stars, because in their case the distance is so enormously greater. The pole star, for example, is believed to be so far off that light, traveling at the inconceivable speed above mentioned, takes a little more than fifty years to reach our eyes; and from that follows the strange but inevitable inference that we see the pole star not as and where it is at the present moment, but as and where it was fifty years ago. If to-morrow some cosmic catastrophe were to shatter the pole star into fragments, we should still see it peacefully shining in the sky all the rest of our lives; our children would grow up to middle age and gather their children about them in turn before the news of that tremendous accident reached any terrestrial eye. In the same way there are other stars so far distant that light takes thousands of years to move from them to us, and with reference to their condition our information is therefore thousands of years behind time.

Suppose we were able to place a man at the distance of 186,000 miles from the earth, and yet endow him with the wonderful faculty of being able from that distance to see what was happening here as clearly as though he were still close beside us. It is evident that a man so placed would see everything a second after the time when it really happened, and so at the present moment he would be seeing what happened a second ago. Double the distance, and he would be two seconds behind time. Remove him to the distance of the sun, and he would look down and watch you doing, not what you **are** doing now, but what you **were** doing eight minutes ago. Carry him away to the pole star, and he would see passing before his eyes the events of fifty years ago; he would be watching the childish gambols of those who at the very same moment were really middle-aged men. Marvelous as this is, it is literally and scientifically true, and cannot be denied. The same idea is taken up and worked out in Camille Flammarion's book, "Stories in Infinity." Our little treatise went on to argue that God, being omnipresent, must be at all these points of view at once, and also at every intermediate point, and that He must certainly possess such a power of sight as we have postulated. Consequently, to His sight everything that has ever happened must be happening now—not as a memory, but as a living fact. Now all this is materialistic enough, and on the plane of purely physical science, and we may therefore be assured that it is not the way in which the memory of the Logos acts; yet it is neatly worked out and absolutely incontrovertible, and it is not without its use, since it gives us a glimpse of some possibilities which otherwise might not occur to us. It does suggest to us that an infinite power must possess faculties which are utterly beyond our grasp, which would produce results far surpassing our wildest efforts of imagination.

PSYCHOMETRIC DELINEATIONS.

But, it may be asked, how is it possible, amid the bewildering confusion of these records of the past, to find any particular picture when it is wanted? As a matter of fact, the untrained clairvoyant usually cannot do so without some special link to put him in touch with the subject required. Psychometry is an instance in point, and it is quite probable that our ordinary memory is really only another presentment of the same idea. It seems as though there were a sort of magnetic attachment or affinity between any particle of matter and the record which contains its history—an affinity which enables it to act as a kind of conductor between that record and the faculties of any one who can read it. For example, I once brought from Stonehenge a tiny fragment of stone, not larger than a pin's head, and on putting this into an envelope and handing it to a psychometer who had no idea what it was, she at once began to describe that wonderful ruin and the desolate country surrounding it, and then went on to picture what were evidently scenes from its early history, showing that that infinitesimal fragment had been sufficient to put her into communication with the records connected with the spot from which it came. It would seem as though the very walls of our rooms were phonographs, which can be made to reproduce to a person trained to understand them, not only the sounds but also the pictures which have been impressed upon them. There is a separate literature of this subject of psychometry, and it is well worth our study. The best book that I know upon it is Professor Denton's "Soul of Things"; and there is also a valuable work by Dr. Rodes Buchanan.

It is quite possible that the human memory may be a phenomenon of the same nature. The old idea was that all the information possessed by a man was simply stored in the cells of his physical brain, but it is very evident that that is not so, because the man has been repeatedly shown to be capable of consciousness and memory when away from his physical brain altogether; though undoubtedly for work on the physical plane the brain is necessary. Still the storage theory seems unlikely; it may be that the scenes through which we pass in the course of our life act in the same manner upon the particles of our mental body as did the history of Stonehenge upon that particle of stone—that they establish a connection by means of which our mind is put en rapport with that particular portion of the record, and so we remember what we have seen.

The student who develops this power of psychometry has a very interesting field of research before him. Not only can he review at his leisure all the history with which we are acquainted, correcting as he examines it the many errors and misconceptions which have crept into the accounts handed down to us; he can also range at will over the whole story of the world from the very beginning, watching the unfolding of the intellect in man through prehistoric ages, and contemplating the glory of mighty civilizations whose very traces have long ago been lost in the mists of time. Sometimes an even closer sympathy with the past is possible for the reader of the records, for he may learn to look back upon his own part in the earlier history of the world; he may awaken the memory of his previous lives, and thus identify himself once more with long-dead personalities. Probably this happens much oftener than we think; many a casual unidentified clairvoyant vision, many a dream of strange, incomprehensible surroundings, may be nothing but a half-recollection of days so very long ago that the world has greatly changed since then. Many among us now are approaching the borderland which divides the physical senses from the astral and we catch glimpses from the other side without recognizing them for what they really are. There are many who possess something of this power of psychometry without being at all aware of it, and they are constantly receiving impressions from letters, from articles of furniture, and from surroundings generally, even though they do not realize the source from which these impressions come.

FORESEEING WHAT HAS NOT HAPPENED.

Even though the average man cannot see exactly how it is done, he may yet readily understand and be prepared to accept the possibility of this impression of past events upon surrounding obects, guided thereto by such partial analogies as the phonograph and the photographic camera. But when we come to face the problem of the second part of our subject, there is for him a much greater difficulty. That which has passed may conceivably have left an impression; but how can that which has not yet happened be foreseen? There is no question at all that this does occur; the authenticated accounts of second sight among the Highlanders of Scotland alone would suffice to demonstrate the fact, even if there were no other evidence. But there is very much other evidence; and no one who has examined the question can doubt that the soul or ego in man possesses a certain power of prevision at his own level. Sometimes he is able to impress what he knows clearly upon his physical brain; sometimes he succeeds only very partially in that effort and probably there are many occasions when he fails altogether to produce his impression, and so in our waking consciousness we know nothing about it, or at most feel only a vague uneasiness or depression.

If the events foreseen were always of great importance, one might suppose that an extraordinary stimulus had enabled him for that occasion only to make a clear impression upon his lower personality. No doubt that is the explanation of many of the cases in which death or grave disaster is foreseen, but there are large numbers of instances on record to which it does not seem to apply, since the events are frequently trivial and unimportant. Let me give you an instance. A man who had no belief in the occult was forewarned by a Highland seer of the approaching death of a neighbor. The prophecy was given with considerable wealth of detail, including a full description of the funeral, with the names of the four pall-bearers and others who would be present. The auditor seems to have laughed at the whole story and promptly forgotten it, but the death of his neighbor at the time foretold recalled the warning to his mind, and he determined to falsify part of the prediction at any rate by being one of the pall-bearers himself. He succeeded in getting matters arranged as he wished, but just as the funeral was about to start he was called away from his post by some small matter which detained him only a minute or two. As he came hurrying back he saw with surprise that the procession had started without him, and that the prediction had been exactly fulfilled, for the four pall-bearers were those who had been indicated in the vision.

Now this was a very trifling matter, which could have been of no possible importance to anybody; yet it was foretold accurately weeks before it occurred, and though a man makes a determined effort to alter the arrangement indicated, he fails to affect it in the least. We can hardly suppose that any soul made a violent endeavor to bring through into his lower consciousness such valueless details as these. What may however have happened is that the ego of the neighbor was anxious to warn his physical manifestation of its approaching death, but found himself unable to affect his brain directly. In such a dilemma he may have impressed the nearest sensitive person (the seer), and in throwing the picture into the mind of that person he may have supplied all the details of the scene, as he naturally would do. But how is this prevision obtained?

TWO METHODS OF PREVISION.

There are two methods by which it may be gained. One of them is clearly comprehensible to us on this physical plane; the other is not so easily explicable, because of the limitations of our consciousness. There is no doubt whatever that, just as what is happening now is the result of causes set in motion in the past, so what will happen in the future will be the result of causes already in operation. Even down here we can calculate that if certain actions are performed certain effects will follow, but our reckoning is constantly liable to be disturbed by the interference of factors which we have not been able to take into account. But if we raise our consciousness to the mental plane we can see very much farther into the results of our actions. In fact, it may be said that at that level the effects of all causes at present in action are plainly visible—that the future, as it would be if no entirely new causes should arise, lies open before our gaze New causes of course do arise, because man's will is free; but in the case of all ordinary people the use which they will make of their freedom can be calculated beforehand with considerable accuracy.

Looking down upon man's life from this level of the mental plane, it seems as though his free will could be exercised only at certain crises in his career. He arrives at a point in his life where there are obviously two or three alternative courses open before him; he is absolutely free to choose which of them he pleases. But when he has chosen, he has to go through with it and take the consequences; having entered upon a particular path he may, in many cases, be forced to go on for a very long way before he has any opportunity to turn aside. His position is somewhat like that of the driver of a train; when he comes to a junction he may conceivably have the points set either this way or that, and so can pass on to whichever line he pleases, but when he has passed on to one of them he is compelled to continue along the line which he has selected until he reaches another set of points (or switches, as I think they are called in this country) where again an opportunity of choice is offered to him.

In looking down from the mental plane, these new points of departure would be clearly visible, and all the results of each choice would lie open before us, certain to be worked out even to the smallest detail. The only point which would remain uncertain would be which of them he would choose. We should, in fact, have not one but several futures mapped out before our eyes, without necessarily being able to determine which of them would materialize itself into accomplished fact. If we knew the man thoroughly well, we might feel almost certain what his choice would be, but of course that knowledge would in no sense be a compelling force. If we have a pet dog, we know fairly well what he will do under certain circumstances, but that does not in the least make him do it. It is quite possible to foresee without compelling and so it may well be that the Deity can absolutely foresee all human action, and yet that He in no way prescribes what that action shall be. He looks down upon us from a level so much higher, that all possible causes must lie open and clear before His sight. At however infinitely lower a level, the soul of man also is in its essence divine, and it shares this god-like faculty of prevision to a very considerable extent; it can see a vast number of causes which are concealed from mortal eye, and so it is sometimes capable of impressing a definite forecast upon its physical brain. This method of prophecy is at any rate quite intelligible, for it is merely an expansion of processes of induction with which we are familiar on the physical plane.

ANOTHER KIND OF PREVISION.

There is, however, another and altogether more exalted kind of prevision which is by no means so readily comprehensible. When a man raises his consciousness to the plane above the mental—that which in Theosophical literature is called the buddhic—no such elaborate process of conscious calculation is necessary, for in some manner which down here is totally inexplicable, the past, the present and the future are there all existing simultaneously. One can only accept this fact, for its cause lies in the faculty of the plane, and the way in which this higher faculty works is naturally quite incomprehensible to the physical brain. Yet now and then we may meet with a hint that seems to bring us a trifle nearer to a dim possibility of comprehension. One such hint was given by Sir Oliver Lodge in an address to the British Association at Cardiff. He said.

"A luminous and helpful idea is that time is but a relative mode of regarding things; we progress through phenomena at a certain definite pace, and this subjective advance we interpret in an objective manner, as if events moved necessarily in this order and at this precise rate. But this may be only one way of regarding them. The events may in some sense be in existence always, and it may be we who are arriving at them, not they which are happening. The analogy of a traveler in a railway train is useful; if he could never leave the train nor alter its pace he would probably consider the landscapes as necessarily successive, and be unable to conceive their co-existence.... we perceive therefore, a possible fourth-dimensional aspect about time, the inexorableness of whose flow may be a natural part of our present limitations. And if we once grasp the idea that past and future may be actually existing, we can recognize that they may have a controlling influence on all present action, and the two together may constitute the 'higher plane' or totality of things after which, as it seems to me, we are compelled to seek, in connection with the directing of form or determinism, and the action of living beings consciously directed to a definite and preconceived end."

Time is not in reality the fourth dimension at all; yet to look at it from that point of view is some slight help towards grasping the ungraspable. Suppose that we hold a wooden cone at right angles to a sheet of paper, and slowly push it through, point first. A microbe living on the surface of that sheet of paper, and having no power of conceiving anything outside of that surface, could not only never see the cone as a whole, but he could form no sort of a conception of such a body at all. All that he would see would be the sudden appearance of a tiny circle, which would gradually and mysteriously grow larger and larger until it vanished from his world as suddenly and incomprehensibly as it had come into it.

Thus what were in reality a series of sections of the cone would appear to him to be successive stages in the life of a circle, and it would be impossible for him to grasp the idea that these successive stages could be seen simultaneously. Yet it is easy enough for us, looking down upon the transaction from another dimension, to see that the microbe is simply under a delusion arising from its own limitations, and that the cone exists as a whole all the while. Our own delusion as to past, present and future is possibly not dissimilar, and the view that is gained of any sequence of events from the buddhic plane corresponds to the view of the cone as a whole; and some glimpse or reflection of that higher consciousness, coming through into our lower world would constitute for us a perfect fragment of prevision. But without experiencing it, it is impossible fully to understand it. How that experience may be gained is the subject which we shall examine in our next lecture.

How to Develop Clairvoyance.

A Lecture Delivered Before a Chicago Audience, by
C. W. Leadbeater, the Great Psychic,
of London, England.

INJURIOUS METHODS—THE USE OF DRUGS—DANCE OF ECSTASY—SELF HYPNOTIZATION—TENNYSON'S EXPERIENCE—REGULATING THE BREATHING—MESMERIC TRANCE—CURATIVE MESMERISM—DESIRABLE METHODS—MENTAL AND MORAL DEVELOPMENT—CONCENTRATION — MEDITATION—CONTEMPLATION.

When a man has studied the subject of clairvoyance sufficiently to realize that the claims made on its behalf are true, his next enquiry usually is, "How can I gain this power for myself? If this faculty be latent in every man, as you say, how can I so develop myself as to bring it into action, and so have direct access to all this knowledge of which you tell me?" In reply we can assure him that this thing can be done, and that it has been done. There are even many ways in which the faculty may be gained, though most of them are unsafe and eminently undesirable, and there is only one that can be thoroughly and unreservedly recommended to all men alike. But that we may understand the subject, and see where lie the dangers that have to be avoided, let us consider exactly what it is that has to be done.

In the case of all cultured people belonging to the higher races of the world, the faculties of the astral body are already fully developed, as I have explained in earlier lectures. But we are not in the least in the habit of using them; they have slowly grown up within us during the ages of our evolution, but they have come to us so gradually that we have not as yet realized our powers, and they are still to a great extent untried weapons in our hands. The physical faculties, to which we are thoroughly accustomed, overshadow these others and hide their very existence, just as the nearer light of the sun hides from our eyes the light of the far-distant stars. So that there are two things to be done if we wish to enter into this part of our heritage as evolved human beings; we must keep our too-insistent physical faculties out of the way for the time, and we must habituate ourselves to the employment of these others, which are as yet unfamiliar to us.

INJURIOUS METHODS.

The first step, then, is to get the physical senses out of the way for the time. There are many ways of doing this, but broadly they all range themselves under two heads—one comprising methods by which they are forced out of the way by temporary violent suppression, and the other including methods much slower but infinitely surer, by which we ourselves gain permanent control over them. Most of the methods of violent suppression are injurious to the physical body, to a greater or less extent, and they all have certain undesirable characteristics in common. One of those is that they leave the man in a passive condition, able perhaps to use his higher senses, but with very little choice as to how he shall employ them, and to a large extent undefended against any unpleasant or evil influence which he may happen to encounter. Another characteristic is that any power gained by these methods can at best be only temporary. Many of them confer it only during the limited period of their action, and even the best of them can only dower the man with certain faculties during this one physical life. In the East, where they have studied these matters for so many centuries, they divide methods of development into two classes, just as I have done, and they call them by the names laukika and lokothra, the first being the "worldly" or temporary method, any results gained by which will inhere only in the personality, and therefore be available only for this present physical life, while whatever is obtained by the second process is gained by the ego, the soul, the true man, and so is a permanent possession for evermore, carried over from one earthly life to another. For most methods of the former class little training is required, and when there is training it is of the vehicles only, and so at the best it can affect only this present set of vehicles, and when the man returns into incarnation with a fresh set all his trouble will be lost; whereas by the second method it is the soul itself which is trained in the control of its vehicles, and naturally it can apply the power and the knowledge thus gained to its new vehicles in the next life. Let me mention to you first some of the undesirable ways in which clairvoyance is developed in various countries.

THE USE OF DRUGS.

Among non-Aryan tribes in India it is often obtained by the use of drugs—bhang, hasheesh and others of the same kind. These stupefy the physical body something as anaesthetics do, and thus the man in his astral vehicle is set free as he would be in sleep, but with far less possibility of being awakened. Before taking the drug, the man has set his mind strongly on the endeavor to train his astral senses into activity, and so as soon as he is free he tries to use his faculties, and with practice he succeeds to some extent. When he awakens his physical body, he remembers more or less of his visions, and tries to interpret them, and in that way he often obtains a great reputation for clairvoyance and prevision. Sometimes while in his trance he may be spoken through by some dead man, just as any other medium may be. There are others who obtain the same condition by inhaling stupefying fumes, usually produced by the burning of a mixture of drugs. It is probable that the clairvoyance of the pythonesses of old was often of this type. It is stated in the case of one of the most celebrated of those oracles of ancient days, the priestess sat always upon a tripod exactly over a crack in the rock, out of which vapor ascended. After breathing this vapor for a time, she became entranced, and some one then spoke through her organs in the ordinary way so familiar to the visitors to seances. It is not difficult for us to see how undesirable both these methods are from the point of view of real development.

DANCE OF ECSTASY.

Probably most of us have heard of the dancing dervishes, one part of whose religion consists in this curious dance of ecstasy, in which they whirl round and round in a kind of frenzy until vertigo seizes them, and they eventually fall insensible to the ground. In that trance, worked up as they are by religious fervor, they frequently have most extraordinary visions, and are able to some extent to experience and remember lower astral conditions. I have seen something of this, and also of the practices of the Obeah or Voodoo votaries among the negroes; but these latter are usually connected with magical ceremonies, loathsome, indecent, horrible, such as none of us would dream of touching for any purpose, whatever results might be promised to us. Yet they certainly do produce results under favorable conditions, though not such results as any of us could possibly wish to obtain. Indeed, none of the methods mentioned so far would at all commend themselves to us, though I have heard of Europeans who have experimented with the Oriental drugs.

SELF HYPNOTIZATION.

Nevertheless we also have undesirable methods in the West—methods of self hypnotization which should be carefully avoided by all who wish to develop in purity and safety. A person may be told to gaze for some time at a bright spot, until paralysis of some of the brain centres supervenes, and in that way he is cast into a condition of perfect passivity, in which it is possible that the lower astral senses may come into a measure of activity. Naturally he has no power of selection in receiving under such circumstances; he must submit himself to whatever comes in his way, good or bad—and on the whole it is much more likely to be bad than good. Sometimes the same general result is obtained by the recitation of certain formulae, the repetition of which over and over again deadens the mental faculty almost as the gazing at a metal disc does. It may be remembered that the poet Tennyson tells us that he was able by the recitation of his own name many times in rapid succession to pass into another condition of consciousness. The account is given in a letter in the poet's handwriting, which is dated Faringford, Freshwater, Isle of Wight, May 7, 1874. It was written to a gentleman who communicated to him certain strange experiences he had when passing from under the effect of anaesthetics. Tennyson says:

TENNYSON'S EXPERIENCE.

"I have never had any revelations through anaesthetics; but a kind of waking trance (this for lack of a better name) I have frequently had, quite up from boyhood, when I have been all alone. This has often come upon me through re-

HOW CLAIRVOYANCE IS DEVELOPED. 31

peating my own name to myself silently, till all at once out of the intensity of the consciousness of individuality, the individuality itself seemed to dissolve and fade away into boundless being; and this not a confused state, but the clearest of the clearest, the surest of the surest, utterly beyond words, where death was an almost laughable impossibility, the loss of personality (if so it were) seeming no extinction, but the only true life. I am ashamed of my feeble description. Have I not said the state is utterly beyond words? This is the most emphatic declaration that the spirit of the writer is capable of transferring itself into another state of existence, is not only real, clear, simple, but that it is also infinite in vision and eternal in duration."

Now here is undoubtedly a touch of the higher life; no one who has practical experience of realities can fail to recognize the description as far as it goes, even though the poet just stops short on the brink of something so infinitely grander. He seems to have held himself more positive than do many people who dabble in these matters without the necessary instruction or knowledge, and so he gained a valuable certainty of the existence of the soul apart from the body; yet even his method cannot be commended as good or really safe.

REGULATING THE BREATHING.

We are sometimes told that such a faculty can be developed by means of exercises which regulate the breathing, and that this plan is one largely adopted and recommended in India. It is true that a type of clairvoyance may be developed along these lines, but too often at the cost of ruin both physical and mental. Many attempts of this sort have been made here in the United States; I know it personally, because on my previous visit many who had ruined their constitutions and in some cases brought themselves to the verge of insanity came to me to know how they could be cured. Some have succeeded in opening astral vision sufficiently to feel themselves perpetually haunted; some have not even reached that point, yet have wrecked their physical health or weakened their minds so that they are in utter despair; some one or two declare that such practice has been beneficial to them. It is true that such exercises are employed in India by the Hatha Yogis—those who attempt to attain development rather by physical means than by inner growth of the mental and the spiritual. But even among them such

Meditative posture used for breathing exercises. Creates a "circuit" of energy within

practices are used only under the direct orders of responsible teachers, who watch the effect upon the pupil of what is prescribed, and will at once stop him if the exercises prove unsuitable for him. But for people who know nothing at all of the subject to attempt such thing indiscriminately is most unwise and dangerous, for practices which are useful for one man may very well be disastrous for another. They may suit one man in fifty, but they are extremely likely not to suit the rest, and myself I should advise every one to abstain from them unless directed to try them by a competent teacher who really understands what they are intended to achieve. You may be the one whom they will suit, but the probabilities are against it, for there are far more failures than successes. It is so fatally easy to do a great deal of harm in this way, that to experiment vaguely is rather like going into a chemist's shop and taking down drugs at random; you might happen to hit upon exactly what you needed, but also you might not, and the latter is many times more probable.

MESMERIC TRANCE.

Another method by which clairvoyance may be developed is by mesmerism—that is to say, if a person be thrown by another into a mesmeric trance it is possible that in that trance he may see astrally. The mesmerizer entirely dominates his will, and the physical faculties are thrown utterly into abeyance. That leaves the field open, and the mesmerist can at the same time stimulate the astral senses by pouring vitality into the astral body. Good results have been produced in this way, but it requires a very unusual combination of circumstances, an almost superhuman development of purity in thought and intention both in the operator and the subject to make the experiment a safe one. The mesmerist gains great influence over his subject—a far greater power than is generally known; and it may be unconsciously exercised. Any quality of heart or mind possessed by the mesmerist is very readily transferred to the subject, so if he be not entirely pure, we see at once that avenues of danger open up before us. To be thrown into a trance is to give up your individuality, and that is never a good thing in psychic experiments; but beyond and above that element of undesirability there is real danger unless you have the highest purity of thought, word and deed in your operator; and how rarely that is to be found you know as well as I do. I should never

Effects of mesmerism, circa 1901

HOW CLAIRVOYANCE IS DEVELOPED.

myself submit to this process; I should never advise it to any one else.

CURATIVE MESMERISM.

I say nothing against the practice of curative mesmerism by those who understand it; that is a totally different matter, for in that it is unnecessary to produce the trance condition at all. It is perfectly possible to relieve pain, to remove disease, or to pour vitality into a man by magnetic passes, without "putting him to sleep" at all. To this there can be no possible objection; yet the man who tries to do even this much would do well to acquaint himself thoroughly with the literature of the subject, for there must always remain a certain element of danger in playing, even with the noblest intentions, with forces which you do not understand, which to you are still abnormal forces. None of these are plans of clairvoyant development which can be unreservedly recommended for trial by every one.

DESIRABLE METHODS.

What, then, it may be asked, are the desirable methods, since so many are undesirable? Broadly, those which instead of suppressing the physical body by force, train the soul to control it. The surest and safest way of all is to put oneself into the hands of a competent teacher, and practice only what he advises. But where is the qualified teacher to be found? Not, assuredly, among any who advertise themselves as teachers; not among those who take money for their instruction, and offer to sell the mysteries of the universe for so many shillings or so many dollars. Knowledge can be gained now where it has always been available—at the hands of those who are adepts in this great science of the soul, the fringe of which we are beginning to touch in our deepest studies. There has always been a great Brotherhood of the men who know, and they have always been ready to teach their lore to the right man, for it is for that very purpose that they have taken the trouble to acquire it, in order that they may be able to guide and help. How can we reach them? You cannot reach them in the physical body, and you might not even know them if it should happen to you to see them. But they can reach you, and assuredly they will reach you when they see you to be fit for the work of helping the world. Their one great interest is the furthering of evolution, the helping of humanity; they need men devoted to this work, and they are ever watching for them; so none need fear that he can be overlooked if he is ready for that work. They will never gratify mere curiosity; they will give no aid to the man who wishes to gain powers for himself alone; but when a man has shown by long and careful training of himself, and by using for helpfulness all the power that he already possesses, that his will is strong enough and his heart pure enough to bear his part in the Divine work—then he may become conscious of their presence and their aid when he least expects it.

It is true that they founded the Theosophical Society, yet membership in the society will not of itself be sufficient to bring a man into relationship with them—no, nor even membership in that Inner School through which the society offers training to its more earnest members. It is true that from the ranks of the society men have been chosen to come into closer relation with them; but none could guarantee that as a result of becoming a member, for it rests with them alone, for they see further into the hearts of men than we. But always be sure of this, you whose hearts are yearning for the higher life, for something greater than this lower world can give, that they never overlook one honest effort, but always recognize it by giving through their pupils such teaching and such help as the man at his stage is ready for.

In the meantime, while you are trying in every way to develope yourselves along the path of progress, there is much that you can do, if you wish, to bring this power of clairvoyance nearer within your reach. Remember that it is not in itself a sign of great development; it is only one of the signs, for man has to advance along many lines simultaneously before he can reach his goal of perfection. See how highly developed is the intellect in the great scientific man; yet perhaps he may have but little yet of the wonderful force which devotion gives. See the splendid devotion of the great saint of some church or religion; yet in spite of all that progress along one line he may have but little yet of the divine power of the intellect. Each needs what the other has; each will have to acquire the faculty of the other before he will be perfect. So it is evident that at present we are unequally developed; some have more in one direction, and some in another, according to the line along which each has worked most in past lives. So if you particularly long for devotion in your character, by striving in that direction now you may attain much of it even in this life, and may assuredly make it

HOW CLAIRVOYANCE IS DEVELOPED.

a leading quality in your next life. So with intellect, so with every quality; so also with this faculty of clairvoyance. If you think it well to throw your strength into work along this line, you may do very much towards bringing these latent faculties into action.. I am not speaking here of a vague possibility, but of a definite fact, for some of our own members in this society set themselves years ago to try to train the soul along the path of permanent progress, and of those who persevered without faltering almost every one has even already found some definite result. Some have won their faculties fully, others only partially as yet, but in all cases good has come from their efforts to take themselves in hand and control their minds and emotions.

MENTAL AND MORAL DEVELOPMENT.

If you have this desire for higher sight, take yourself in hand first in the same way; make sure first of the mental and moral development, lest you should succeed in your efforts, and gain your powers. For to possess them without having first acquired those other qualifications would be indeed a curse and not a blessing, for you would then misuse them, and your last state would indeed be worse than the first. If you consider that you have made sure of yourself, and can trust yourself under all possible circumstances to do the right for right's sake, even against your earthly seeming interest, always to choose the utterly unselfish course of action, and to forget yourself in your love for the world, then there are at least two methods which will lead you towards clairvoyance safely, and can in no way do you harm, even though you should not succeed in your object. The first of these, though perfectly harmless and even useful, is not suited for every one; but the second is of universal application, and I have myself known both of them to be successful.

This first method is a purely intellectual one, a study to which I have already on several occasions had to refer, the study of the Fourth Dimension of space. The physical brain has never been accustomed to act at all along those lines, and so it feels itself unable to attack such a problem. But the brain, like any other part of the physical organism, can be trained by persistent, gradual, careful effort to feats which appeared originally quite beyond its reach, and so it can be induced to understand and conceive clearly the forms of a world unlike its own. The chief apostle of the fourth dimension is Mr. C. H. Hinton, of Washington, D. C. He is not a member of our society, but he has done many of its members an excellent piece of service in writing so clearly and luminously on his wonderful subject. In his books he tells us that he has himself succeeded in developing this power of higher conception in the physical brain, and several of our own members have followed in his footsteps. One of these has developed astral sight simply by steadily raising the capacity of the physical brain until it contained the possibility of grasping astral form, and thus awakening the latent astral faculty proper. It is simply a question of extending the power of receptivity until it includes the astral matter. But I suppose that out of a score of men who took up this study, not more than one would succeed as well and as quickly as that; but at any rate the study is a most fascinating one for those who have a mathematical turn of mind, and where it does not bring increased faculty to see, it must at least bring wider comprehension and a broader outlook over the world, and this is no mean result, even if no other be attained. Short of absolute astral sight, it is the only method of which I know by which a clear comprehension can be gained of the appearance of astral objects, and thus a definite idea of what the astral life really is.

If that line of effort commends itself only to the few, our second method is of universal application. It also is not easy, but its practice cannot but be of the greatest use to the man. That is its great and crowning advantage; it leads a man towards these powers which he so ardently desires; but the rate at which he can move along that road depends upon the degree of his previous development in that particular way in other lines, and therefore no one can guarantee him a certain result in a certain time; yet while he is working his way onward, every step which he takes is so far an improvement, and even though he should work for the whole of his life without winning astral sight, he would nevertheless be mentally and morally and even physically the better for having tried. This is what in various religions is called the method of meditation. For the purpose of our examination of it I shall divide it into three successive steps: concentration, meditation and contemplation, and I will explain what I mean by each of these three terms.

But remember always that to attain success, this effort must be only one side of a general development, and that it is absolutely prerequisite for the man who would learn its-

HOW CLAIRVOYANCE IS DEVELOPED. 37

secrets to live a pure and altruistic life. There is no secret about the rules of the greater progress; the Steps of the Path of Holiness have been known to the world for ages, and in my little book, "Invisible Helpers," I have given a list of them according to the teaching of the Buddha, with the characteristics which mark each of its stages. There is no difficulty in knowing what to do; the difficulty is in carrying out the directions which all religions have given.

CONCENTRATION.

The first step necessary towards the attainment of the higher clairvoyance is concentration—not to gaze at a bright spot until you have no mind left, but to acquire such control over your mind that you can do with it what you will, and fix it exactly where you want to hold it for as long a period as you choose. This is not an easy task, it is one of the most difficult and arduous known to man; but it can be done, because it has been done—not once, but hundreds of times, by those whose will is strong and immovable. There may be some among us who have never thought how much beyond our control our minds usually are. Stop yourself suddenly when you are walking along the street, or when you are riding in the car, and see what you are thinking, and why. Try to follow the thought back to its genesis, and you will probably be surprised to find how many desultory thoughts have wandered through your brain during the previous five minutes, just dropping in and dropping out again, and leaving almost no impression. You will gradually begin to realize that in truth all these are not your thoughts at all, but simply cast-off fragments of other people's thoughts. The fact is that thought is a force, and every exertion of it leaves an impression behind. A strong thought about some other person goes to him, a strong thought of self clings about the thinker; but so many thoughts are not by any means strong or especially pointed in any direction, and so the forms which they create are vaguely-floating and evanescent. While they last they are capable of entering into any mind that happens to come their way, and so it comes that as we walk along the road we leave a trail of feeble thought behind us, and the next man who passes that way finds these valueless fragments intruding themselves upon his consciousness. They drift into his mind, unless it is already occupied with something definite, and in the majority of cases they just drift out again, having made only the most trifling impression upon his brain; but here and there he encounters one which interests or pleases him, and then he takes that up and turns it over in his mind, so that it departs from him somewhat strengthened by the addition of a little of his mind-force to it. He has made it his own thought for a moment, and so has colored it with his personality. Every time we enter a room we step into the midst of a crowd of thoughts, good, bad or indifferent as the case may be, but the great mass of them just a dull, purposeless fog which is hardly worth calling thought at all.

If we wish to develop any higher faculty, we must begin by gaining control over this mind of ours. We must give it some work to do, instead of just letting it play about as it will, drawing into itself all these thoughts which are not ours, which we really do not want at all. It must be not our master but our servant before we can take the first step along the line of the true trained clairvoyance, for this is the instrument which we shall have to use, and it must be at our command and fully under our control.

This concentration is one of the hardest things for the ordinary man to do, because he has had no practice at it, and indeed has scarcely realized that it needed to be done. Think what it would be if your hand were as little under your control as your mind is, if it did not obey your command, but started aside from what you wished it to do. You would feel that you had paralysis, and that your hand was useless. But if you cannot control your mind, that is dangerously like a mental paralysis; you must practice with it until you have it in hand and can use it as you wish. Fortunately concentration can be practiced all day long, in the common affairs of every-day life. Whatever you are doing, do it thoroughly, and keep your mind on it. If you are writing a letter, think of your letter and of nothing else until it is finished; it will be all the better written for such care. If you are reading a book, fix your mind on it and try to grasp the author's full meaning. Know always what you are thinking about, and why; keep your mind at intelligent work, and do not leave it time to be so idle, for it is in those idle moments that all evil comes.

Even now you can concentrate very perfectly when your interest is sufficiently keenly excited. Then your mind is so entirely absorbed that you hardly hear what is said to you or see what passes round you. There is a story told in the East about some skeptical courtiers, who declined to be-

HOW CLAIRVOYANCE IS DEVELOPED.

lieve that an ascetic could ever be so occupied with his meditation as to be unaware that an army passed close by him as he sat under his tree wrapt in thought. The king, who was present, assured them that he would prove to them the possibility of this, and proceeded to do so in a truly Oriental and autocratic way. He ordered that some large water-jars should be brought and filled to the brim. Then he instructed the courtiers each to take one and carry it; and his command was that they should walk, carrying this water, through the principal streets of the city. But they were to be surrounded by his guards with drawn swords, and if one of them spilled one single drop of his water, that unfortunate was to be instantly beheaded then and there. The courtiers started on their journey filled with terror; but they all got safely back again, and the king smilingly greeted them with a request to tell him all the incidents of their walk, and describe the persons whom they had met. Not one of them could mention even one person that they had seen, for all agreed that they had been so entirely occupied with the one idea of watching the brimming jars that they had noticed nothing else of any sort. "So, gentleman," rejoined the king, "you see that when there is sufficient interest concentration is possible."

MEDITATION.

When you have attained concentration such as that, not under the stress of the fear of instant death, but by the exertion of your will, then you may profitably try the next stage of effort. I do not say that it will be easy; on the contrary, it is very difficult; but it can be done, for many of us have had to do it. When your mind is thus an instrument, try what we call meditation. Choose a certain fixed time for yourself, when you can be undisturbed; the early morning is in many ways the best, if that can be managed. It is not always an easy time for us now, for we have in modern civilization hopelessly disarranged our day, so that noon is no longer its middle point, as it should be. Now we lie in bed long after the sun has risen, and then stay up, injuring our eyes with artificial light long after he has set at night. But choose your time, and let it be the same time each day, and let no day pass without your regular effort. You know if you are trying any sort of physical exercise for training purposes how much more effective it is to do a little regularly than to make a violent effort one day, and then do nothing for a week. So in this matter it is the regularity that is important.

Sit down comfortably where you will not be disturbed, and turn your mind, with all its newly-developed power of concentration, upon some selected subject demanding high and useful thought. We in our Theosophical studies have no lack of such subjects, combining deepest interest with greatest profits. If you prefer it, you can take some moral quality, as is advised by the Catholic church when it prescribes this exercise. In that case, you would turn the quality over in your mind, see how it was an essential quality in the Divine order, how it was manifested in Nature about you, how it had been shown forth by great men of old, how you yourself could manifest it in your daily life, how (perhaps) you have failed to display it in the past, and so on. Such meditation upon a high moral quality is a very good exercise in many ways, for it not only trains the mind, but keeps the good thought constantly before you. But it needs to be preceded generally by thought upon concrete subjects, and when those are easy for you, you can usefully take up the more abstract ideas.

CONTEMPLATION.

When this has become an established habit with you, with which nothing is allowed to interfere; when you can manage it fairly well without any feeling of strain or difficulty, and without a single wandering thought ever venturing to intrude itself; then you may turn to the third stage of our effort—contemplation. But remember that you will not succeed with this until you have entirely conquered the mind-wandering. For a long time you will find, when you try to meditate, that your thoughts are continually going off at a tangent, and you do not know it till suddenly you start to find how far away they have gone. You must not let this dishearten you, for it is the common experience; you must simply bring the errant mind back again to its duty, a hundred or a thousand times if necessary, for the only way to succeed is to decline to admit the possibility of failure. But when you have at length succeeded, and the mind is definitely mastered, then we reach that for which all the rest has been but the necessary preparation, good though it has also been in itself.

Instead of turning over a quality in your mind, take the highest spiritual ideal that you know. It does not matter

HOW CLAIRVOYANCE IS DEVELOPED. 41

what it is, or by what name you call it. A Theosophist would most probably take one of those Great Ones to whom we have already referred—a member of that great Brotherhood of Adepts, whom we call the Masters—especially if he had the privilege of having come directly into contact with one of them. The Catholic might take the Blessed Virgin, or some patron saint; the ordinary Christian would probably take the Christ; the Hindu would perhaps choose Krishna, and the Buddhist most likely the Lord Buddha himself. Names do not matter, for we are dealing with realities now. But it must be to you the highest, that which will evoke in you the greatest feeling of reverence, love and devotion that you are capable of experiencing. In place of your previous meditation, call up the most vivid mental image that you can make of this ideal, and, letting your most intense feeling go out towards this highest One, try with all the strength of your nature to raise yourself towards Him, to become one with Him, to be in and of that glory and beauty. If you will do that, if you will thus steadily continue to raise your consciousness, there will come a time when you will suddenly find that you are one with that ideal as you never were before, when you realize and understand Him as you never did before, for a new and wonderful light has somehow dawned for you, and all the world is changed, for now for the first time you know what it is to live, all life before seems like darkness and death to you as compared with this.

Then it will all slip away again, and you will return to the light of common day—and darkness indeed will appear by comparison. But go on working at your contemplation, and presently that glorious moment will come again and yet again; and each time it will stay with you longer, till there comes a period when that higher life is yours always, no longer a flash or a glimpse of paradise, but a steady glow, a new and never-ceasing marvel every day of your existence. Then for you day and night will be one continuous consciousness, one beautiful life of happy work for the helping of others; yet this, which seems so indescribable and so unsurpassable, is only the beginning of the entrance into the heritage in store for you and for every child of man. Look about you with that new and higher sight, and you will see and grasp many things which until now you have never even suspected —unless, indeed, you have previously familiarized yourself with the investigations of your predecessors along this path.

Continue your efforts, and you will rise higher still, and in due course there will open before your astonished eyes a life as much grander than the astral as that is than the physical, and once more you will feel that the true life has been unknown to you until now; for all the while you are rising nearer to the One Life which alone is perfect Truth and perfect Beauty.

This is a development that must take years, you will say. Yes, that is probable, for you are trying to compress into one life the evolution which would normally spread itself over many; but it is far more than worth the time and the effort. No man can say how long it will take in any individual case, for that depends upon two things—the amount of crust that there is to break through, and the energy and determination that is put into the work. I could not promise you that in so many years you would certainly succeed; I can only tell you that many have tried before you, and that many have succeeded. All the great Masters of Wisdom were once men at our own level; as they have risen, so must we rise. Many of us in our humbler way have tried also, and have succeeded, some more and some less; but none who has tried regrets his attempt, for whatever he has gained, be it little or much, is gained for all eternity, since it inheres in the soul which survives death. Whatever we gain thus we possess in full power and consciousness, and have it always at our command; for this is no mediumship, no feeble intermittent trance-quality, but the power of the developed and glorified life which is to be that of all humanity some day.

But the man who wishes to try to unfold these faculties within himself will be very ill-advised if he does not take care first of all to have utter purity of heart and soul, for that is the first and greatest necessity. If he is to do this, and to do it well, he must purify the mental, the astral and the physical; he must cast aside his pet vices and his physical impurities; he must cease to defile his body with meat, with alcohol or tobacco, and try to make himself pure and clean all through, on this lower plane as well as on the higher ones. If he does not think it worth giving up petty uncleannesses for the higher life, that is exclusively his own affair; it was said of old that one could not serve God and Mammon simultaneously. I do not say that bad habits on the physical plane will prevent him altogether from any psychic development, but I do very emphatically and distinctly say that the man who remains unclean is never free from danger, and that to touch holy things with impure hands is to risk a terrible peril. The man who would try for the higher must free his mind from worry and from lower cares; while doing his duty to the uttermost, he must do it impersonally and for the right's sake, and leave the result in the hands of higher powers. So will he draw round him pure and helpful entities as he moves onward, and will himself radiate sunlight on those in suffering or in sorrow. So shall he remain master of himself, pure and clean and unselfish, using his new powers never for a personal end, but ever for the advancement and the succor of men his brothers, that they also, as they can, may learn to live the wider life, may learn to rise from amid the mists of ignorance and selfishness into the glorious sunlight of the peace of God.

Use and Abuse of Psychic Powers.

A Lecture Delivered Before a Chicago Audience by C. W. Leadbeater, the Great Psychic, of London, England.

TRAINED AND UNTRAINED MAN—PSYCHIC POWERS—USES AND ABUSES—MIND CURE—CLAIRVOYANCE—POWER OF THOUGHT—THOUGHT FORMS—SENSITIVENESS—SENSITIVENESS MISUSED.

Strictly speaking psychic powers mean the powers of the soul because this word psychic is derived from the Greek psuche, the soul. But in ordinary language this term is used rather to imply what we in Theosophy should call the powers of the astral body, or even in many cases those pertaining to the etheric part of the physical body. To speak of persons as "psychic" generally means nothing more than that they are sensitive—that they sometimes see or hear more than the majority of people around them are as yet able to see or hear. Though it is of course true that this sight is a power of the soul, it is equally true that all the powers which we display in physical life are also powers of the soul, for our bodies, whether astral or physical, are after all only vehicles. What is commonly termed "psychic power" is then only a very slight extension of ordinary faculties; but the expression is also sometimes used to include other manifestations which are as yet somewhat abnormal among men, such as mesmeric power, or the power of mind cure. Since the will is undoubtedly a quality of the ego, and since that is the motive force both in mesmerism and in mind cure, I presume that we can hardly object to the application of this term psychic power in these cases. Very often telepathy and psychometry are considered to come under the same head, although these in reality merely indicate a somewhat unusual sensitiveness to impressions from without. In reality all of these powers of the soul are inherent in every son of man, though they are developed as yet only in a few, and are working only very partially even with them, unless they have had the inestimable advantage of definite occult training.

TRAINED AND UNTRAINED MAN.

In my lectures upon Clairvoyance I have very often had to draw a decided distinction between the trained and the untrained man. Until we come to examine the matter practically we can have very little idea what an enormous difference the definite training in the use of such powers really makes to the capacity of the man. Practically all those of whom we commonly think of as psychic in this occidental country are entirely untrained. They are simply persons who possess a little of this higher faculty, which has been born in them as a consequence of some efforts which they have made to attain it in past lives—possibly as vestal virgins in ancient temples, or possibly as practitioners of less desirable forms of magic in medieval times. In most cases in this life they have used such powers somewhat blindly, or perhaps have made no conscious effort to use them at all, but have rather been satisfied to accept whatever impressions came to them. In India, and in other Oriental countries, these things have been scientifically studied for very many centuries, so that there any one who shows signs of such development is instructed either to repress its manifestations altogether, or else put himself under the definite training of those who thoroughly understand the subject. The Indian mind approaches these problems from a totally different point of view. To the Hindu more sensitiveness seems an undesirable quality lest it should degenerate into mediumship—a condition which he regards with the utmost horror. To him these powers of the soul do not seem in the slightest degree abnormal; he knows that they are inherent in every man, and so he is in no way surprised at their occasional manifestation. But he knows also that unless carefully trained and kept in perfect control they are very liable to mislead their possessor in the early days of his experiences.

The Indian student knows what he is doing in regard to these matters, for they have all thoroughly classified thou-

USE AND ABUSE OF PSYCHIC POWERS. 47

sands of years ago. There are many teachers in India who will take a man and train him quite definitely, just as here a man might be trained in athletics or in the practice of some science. You will readily realize therefore that in Eastern countries the whole thing is systematized in a way very different from that which prevails among us. All of those whom here you call psychic and clairvoyant would be regarded in the East as not very promising pupils. Indeed I believe that many of the Oriental teachers would rather not undertake the development of a man who has already some small amount of these psychic powers, because it is found that such a man has usually much to unlearn, and is far more difficult to manage and to train than one in whom as yet no such faculties have manifested themselves. In the East they have a thorough comprehension of all these things, and therefore fewer mistakes are likely to occur among them; for with them a man is trained in the use of his faculties from the first, and the possibility of error and miscalculation are clearly explained to him and therefore he is naturally far less likely to fall a victim to them.

We know very well how in our Western countries clairvoyance has a bad reputation, by reason of the fact that there are many pretenders to its possession who are constantly unsuccessful and blundering in their efforts. There may be some of these who are simply and entirely impostors; but I imagine that the majority have really some very partial development of this faculty, although they have often entirely misunderstood even the little that they have. Certainly no man in the East would ever come before the public, or be known in any way as a clairvoyant, until he had been trained very far on the way, so that he had passed beyond all possibility of the ordinary gross errors which are so painfully common among so-called clairvoyants here. If you grasp this fact, you will at once see how great is the difference between the trained and the untrained, and how very little reliance is usually to be placed upon the latter.

I know that most psychics among us feel themselves to be infallible, and consider that the messages and impressions which reach them come always from the very highest possible quarters; but the truth is that a very little common sense and study of the subject would show them that in this they are mistaken. No doubt it is to a certain extent gratifying to one's subtle self-conceit to suppose that one has the exclusive power of communication with some great archangel; but if one will but take the trouble to read the literature of the subject it will soon become apparent that many hundreds of other people have also had their private archangels, and have nevertheless been very frequently grossly mistaken. Of course no trained man could possibly fall into such an error as this; but then as I have said the vast majority of our psychics in Europe and America are simply entirely untrained. Some of them may receive a certain amount of guidance from dead people—"spirit guides," as they are often called—but it is very rarely of a definite and practical kind, and it usually tends much more towards mediumship and general sensitiveness than towards the gain of definite control and self development.

I doubt very much whether any large number of our occidental psychics would for a moment submit themselves to the kind of training which the wiser teachers of the East consider necessary. There a man has to try persistently, patiently, over and over again at the very simplest feats until he succeeds in producing his results neatly and perfectly; he is expected to build up his knowledge of higher planes step by step from those with which he is already familiar, and he is not encouraged in lofty flights which take his feet away from the bed-rock of ascertained fact. Our Western psychics would probably consider themselves much injured if they were made to work laboriously at self-control in the way it is always exacted as a matter of course in all Oriental schools of development of these psychic powers.

I suppose that many people would include among psychic powers Astrology, Palmistry and Phrenology. I think, however, that we are hardly justified in describing these as psychic, because in all of them the theory is that the results are obtained by deduction from matters of fact and of observation. The Astrologer ascertains the position of the stars at any given moment, and from that he casts his horoscope or sets up his figure, and after that it is supposed to be a mere matter of calculation to discover what influences are at work. In the same way the Palmist simply observes the lines of the hand and then gives his delineation according to the accepted rules of his science; and the same is done by the Phrenologist from his examination of the varied configuration of the skull. Of course I know that in all these sciences the real proficiency lies in the capacity to balance the contradictory indications and to judge accurately between them; and I am sure that many practitioners of these arts are aided in such decision by impressions which come very much nearer to psychic faculty. To these last perhaps we might permit the name of psychic power, but hardly to the sciences themselves; so that I think we may put them on one side for the purposes of our lecture. It sometimes happens that one who practices some of these arts is in the habit of receiving impressions and communications from some astral entity—impressions which very greatly assist him in judging accurately from the facts put before him. In that case obviously such success as he may attain is not in consequence of his own psychic powers, but of the additional discernment which ordinary astral faculty gives to his departed helper.

In the same way it does not seem to me that mediumship should be recognized among psychic powers, or indeed considered properly a power at all. The man who is a medium is not exercising power, but is on the contrary abdicating his rightful possession of control over his own organs or principles. It is essential for a medium that he should be one whose principles are readily separable. If he is a trance or a writing medium, that means that any astral entity may readily take possession of his physical body and utilize either the hand or the vocal organs, so that he is simply one who can be very readily dispossessed by a dead man. If, on the other hand, he is a materializing medium, whether the materializations are perfect and visible forms, or merely invisible hands which touch the sitters at the seance, or play musical instruments or carry small objects about, then the quality which he possesses is simply that etheric or even physical matter can very readily be withdrawn from his body and used for the various operations of the seance. In any or all of these cases it will be seen that the medium's part is to be passive and not active, and that he may very readily be seized upon and obsessed. So that it is very evident that he cannot be described as possessing or using a power at all, but simply as able to assume a condition in which he can very readily yield himself to the power of others.

PSYCHIC POWERS.

It would seem then that we may reserve the title of "psychic" powers for the definite use of will or of the astral or etheric senses—that is to say that we may include genuine and controlled clairvoyance, mind-cure, mesmerism, telepathy and psychometry. A great deal of unconscious psychic power is also being constantly exercised, and of that I shall speak later; but we will take the conscious exercise of powers first. The conscious exercise of these powers is only for the few among us at present. It is by no means uncommon to find men who have considerable mesmeric capability; and a very fair number of persons possess a good deal of curative power along various lines; but still as compared to the total population these are only a very few. The unconscious powers are possessed by all of us, and all of us are using them to a greater or less extent.

To those then who possess and employ these conscious psychic powers I would say that all of them may be used and all of them may be abused, so that it is very necessary that great care should be exercised with regard to them. There is a very good general rule which is universally applicable with regard to all such matters, and that is the rule of perfect unselfishness. If those who possess such powers are using them in any way for personal gain, whether it be of money or of influence, then that is distinctly an abuse. These are truly powers of the soul; they are connected with the advancement of man and with his higher development, and it is for that higher development only that they should be employed. That is a very important point for the person possessing these powers to bear in mind; it is the only absolutely safe rule that can be made for their use.

These are in all cases glimpses of the future of the human race. If these higher powers which will one day come to everyone of us are to be used by each man for himself, then that future will be a very fearful one and a very dark one. If, on the other hand, as these powers develop men learn to use them for the uplifting and the helping of the race, then that future will be a bright and a grand one. Our record tells us that in the remote past there was a mighty race which possessed those powers to the full; but that race, as a whole used them wrongly, and in consequence that race disappeared. We of the fifth root race must also in our turn pass through the same trial, we must inherit the same powers. Their occasional appearance among us now is an earnest of the time when they will presently become universal, when they will be widely understood and widely accepted.

The great question is whether having followed our predecessors so far, we shall follow them to the end, whether when we have developed these powers as they did, we also shall abuse them as they did; for if we do that, then it is cer-

USE AND ABUSE OF PSYCHIC POWERS.

tain that we shall also follow them in their destruction. But if, as may be hoped, we shall do somewhat better than they, if there shall be a larger proportion who will use these powers for the good of mankind as a whole, then it may be that the doom can be averted, and that the common sense and public feeling of the majority will condemn and curb their employment for selfish purposes But if that is to be, if we are to have this larger proportion of those who understand and who use their powers intelligently, it is certain that we must begin now; now that these things are as yet only in seed among us we must begin by using them unselfishly, and we must put away altogether the idea of exploiting them for the sake of the lower self. There is already very far too great a tendency in this direction; the grasping avarice of the ignorant leads them to employ every additional advantage which they think they can gain, in order that they may make a little more money, that they may obtain a little more advancement or a little more fame for the wretched personal self. The dawn of these higher faculties must never be corrupted by such thoughts or such feelings as these.

We must remember that these higher powers involve higher responsibility, that the man who possesses them is already in a different position, because he is already coming within reach of higher possibilities in many directions. We understand this very readily in other and more purely physical matters, and none of us would think of regarding the responsibility of the savage when he commits a murder or a robbery as in any way equal to our own if we should fall into the same crime. That is simply because we have a greater knowledge than he, and so every one instinctively realizes that more is to be expected from us. Obviously exactly the same thing is true with regard to the question of this additional knowledge—this knowledge that brings with it so much more of power; for added power means added opportunity and therefore added responsibility.

USES AND ABUSES.

In previous lectures I have already explained the Theosophical view with regard to mesmerism and mind cure, so that I need not now repeat myself with regard to these subjects. It is very easy to see how the former might be misused—how it might be employed with great facility to dominate the mind of a person and so to influence him unduly to favor the operator. One hears sometimes of such cases in which a man desiring to obtain a position, or another one desiring to obtain money, will exercise undue mesmeric influence and so get himself appointed to some place which he is obviously unfitted to fill, or perhaps succeed in having money given to him or left to him as a legacy when it should obviously by ordinary canons of justice have passed into quite other hands. It is quite common to see advertisements in the papers of those who profess to teach mesmeric influences avowedly with the intention that it shall be used in ordinary business, in order that the person who uses it may in this way get the better of the unfortunate man who came into contact with him in the way of trade. It is at once obvious that all these are very serious abuses; and I think that we must certainly class with them that use of mesmeric power which is so frequently exhibited in public—that which makes the subject ridiculous in some one or other of many ways. On the other hand there is no doubt that mesmerism may be very usefully and profitably employed for curative purposes. As I explained in my lecture on that subject it is usually possible to withdraw from a patient such pains as those of headache or toothache by means of a few passes without putting him into a trance condition at all. Indeed I imagine that a very large number of the ills to which flesh is heir could be cured in this way without the use of the trance. This latter should be used very sparingly, because it involves domination of one man's will by another. Perhaps almost the only case in which it is undoubtedly justifiable is that of a surgical operation. We shall find many accounts of its successful employment in such cases in the works of Dr. Esdaile of Calcutta, and Dr. Elliotson of London.

MIND CURE.

One may see equally readily how easy it would be to misuse the power of mind cure. It is often employed simply as a means of making money; and it seems to me that wherever that is done there is a terrible danger of impurity in the motive and unscrupulousness in the practice. I know that it will be said that those who devote the whole of their time and strength to the curing of others must themselves obtain their livelihood in some way, and that in this respect mind cure stands on the same level as ordinary medicine. I do not feel myself able to agree with this latter contention. In the case of the ordinary doctor we all know that he has passed through an expensive training in order to fit himself to deal with the especial needs of the human body; and we all realize what it is that we are buying from him—the services which his skill and experience enable him to place at our disposal. But the mind-curist is often entirely ignorant, and has undergone no preliminary training whatever; and in any case he is using a power which cannot be measured upon the physical plane, because it belongs in reality to something higher and less material. If such a practitioner has no means of his own, and is devoting the whole of his time to the work of curing diseases, there can be no objection to his accepting any gift that a grateful patient may wish to make to him in recognition of the help which he has given; but it certainly seems to me that to fix a definite charge for services of this nature is eminently undesirable and contrary to the whole spirit of occult teaching. This is a matter which every person must decide with his own conscience; but it is assuredly a most dangerous thing to introduce any element of personal gain into the utilization of powers which belong to these higher levels. It is certainly better to avoid in this case the very appearance of evil.

CLAIRVOYANCE.

All this is true also of clairvoyance. Most undoubtedly any faculty of that nature which a person possesses may be used for good in a great many ways. For one who possesses this faculty higher worlds lie partially open, at any rate sometimes, and therefore this power may be used to learn. For this purpose it is necessary that the clairvoyant should make a very careful study of the literature of the subject, in order that he may see what others possessing this faculty have previously learnt, that he may be guided by their experience and may avoid the pitfalls into which some of them have fallen. Naturally a clairvoyant who does not study the subject, who makes no effort to verify his visions and to compare them with the experiences of others, is liable to be very seriously deceived, and by his wild predictions and descriptions to bring the whole subject into discredit with those who do not understand it. But for one who uses this power with common sense and without self-conceit, in a scientific spirit of investigation rather than with the hope of obtaining personal gain from it, it may be a source not only of very great pleasure but also of great advancement. Not only may he obtain knowledge for himself—knowledge which he can also pass on to his fellow man, but by its means he may also learn to see when and how people need help, and to distinguish the way in which it can most successfully be given. By its means he can often see where a kind word is especially needed, where a loving, comforting, strengthening thought can be sent with the certainty of immediate result.

The clairvoyant has at least a little more power for good than his fellows if he will only watch for opportunities for using it, if only he will think always of helping others rather than of gaining anything for himself. Beautiful possibilities open up before us when we think of the power that will be in the hands of all in the not far distant future; the man who is to some extent clairvoyant now is beginning already to reap a little of the harvest of power for good which will come to us all as the race advances. So that the clairvoyant who is thoroughly unselfish and whose additional powers are carefully balanced by strong and robust common sense may do a great deal of good in the world and may gain spiritual advancement for himself in the very act of helping his fellow creatures.

It is not difficult to see that this is a power that may be terribly misused. The additional information about others which it puts in the hands of its possessor may be employed, and unfortunately is employed sometimes, for personal gain, for the gratification of curiosity and even for the levying of blackmail. You see from this how essentially necessary it is that the clairvoyant should possess the characteristics of a gentleman, and where he belongs to the class which in Theosophy we call the first-class pitri this is of course the case. But unfortunately clairvoyance may be acquired by less developed souls who do not possess the instincts of the man of delicate feeling, as you may very readily see by some of the disgraceful advertisements which so frequently appear in our papers. There you will see persons quite shamelessly announcing that they are prepared to put clairvoyant power (such as it is) at your disposal in order to help you to obtain an unfair advantage over your fellows in some speculation— that they will help you to rob other men under the pretext of gambling or of betting on horse racing. In this way they are pandering to the lowest passions of man, they are descending from what should be a higher and purer realm into the foulest mud of the most degraded physical life. Nor are these the only offenders, for you will often see announcements from those who profess to teach clairvoyance or occult science of some sort in return for so many pounds or so many dollars. These unscrupulous practitioners are able to live and to flourish simply because the public is as yet entirely ignorant of the true conditions of all such teaching. You may take it as an absolutely certain rule that no true occultist has ever yet advertised himself, and that no true occultist has ever yet taken money for occult teaching or information. The moment that a man advertises—the moment that he takes money for any service which professes to be of an occult nature—that moment he brands himself as having no true occultism to give. True teaching along these lines is to be obtained only from recognized schools of occultism existing under the guardianship of the great Brotherhood; and every pupil of these is absolutely forbidden to take money for the use of any psychic power. So that all these people condemn themselves, and bear this condemnation on the very face of their announcements; and if they flourish and grow fat upon the property of those whom they deceive, the sufferers have only themselves to thank for the results of their own foolish credulity. Once more I repeat that there is one, and only one, absolutely safe rule with regard to the use of all these higher faculties, and that is that they shall never under any conditions be employed for any selfish or personal object.

POWER OF THOUGHT.

Let us turn now from those powers which belong only to the few to those others which all of us possess and are using, even though we may be entirely unconscious of them. The first and the greatest of these is the power of our thought. Many a man has heard vaguely that thoughts are things, and yet the statement has not conveyed to him any very real or definite meaning. When he is fortunate enough to have developed clairvoyance to the level of the mental plane he will be able very fully to bear testimony to the enormous importance of the truth which is expressed in that statement. If, utilizing the senses of the mental body, he looks out through them at the mental bodies of his fellows, he will see how thought manifests itself at that level and what results it produces. It is in the mental body or mind of man that thought first manifests itself; and it shows itself to clairvoyant vision as a vibration arising in the matter of that body. From the plates which I have published in "Man Visible and Invisible" it may be seen what is the appearance of this mental body to the man who is able to see it—or rather what is indicated there is an attempt to present in section and on the physical plane something of the higher and far grander and wider impression which is really made on the sense at that higher level by the appearance of that body.

If a man thinks while the clairvoyant is watching him, the latter will see that a vibration is set up in the mental body and that this vibration produces two distinct results. First of all, like all other vibrations, it tends to communicate itself to any surrounding matter which is capable of receiving it; and thus, since the surrounding atmosphere is filled with mental matter, which is very readily set in motion in response to any such impulse, the first effect produced is that of a sort of ripple which spreads out through surrounding space, exactly as when a stone is thrown into a pond ripples will be seen to radiate from that centre along the surface of the water. In this case the radiation is not in one plane only but in all directions, like the radiation from the sun or from a lamp. It must be remembered that man exists in a great sea of mental matter, just precisely as we here on the physical plane are living in the midst of the atmosphere, although we so rarely think of it. This thought-vibration, therefore, radiates out in all directions, becoming less powerful in proportion to the distance from its source. Again like all other vibrations, this one tends to reproduce itself wherever opportunity is offered to it; and as each variety of thought is represented by its own rate of vibration, that fact means that whenever this wave strikes upon another mental body it will tend to provoke in it vibrations precisely similar to those which gave it birth in the first place. That is to say from the point of view of that other man whose mental body is touched by the wave, it tends to produce in his mind a thought identical with that which had previously arisen in the mind of the thinker. The distance to which such a thought-wave would penetrate, the strength and persistence with which it would impinge upon the mental bodies of others, depends upon the strength and clearness of the original thought.

The voice of a speaker sets in motion waves of sound in the air which radiate from him in all directions, and convey his message to all those who are, as we say, within hearing; and the distance to which his voice can penetrate depends upon its strength and the clearness of his enunciation. In exactly the same way the strong thought will carry very much further than the weak and undecided one; but clearness and definiteness are of even greater importance than strength. But just as the speaker's voice may fall upon heedless ears where men are already engaged in business or in pleasure, so may a strong wave of thought sweep past without affecting the mind of a man if he is already deeply engrossed in some other line of thought. Very large numbers of men, however, do not think very definitely or strongly except when in the immediate prosecution of some business which demands their whole attention. Consequently there are always very many minds within our reach which are liable to be considerably affected by the thoughts which impinge upon them; and we therefore are very distinctly responsible for the thoughts which we send out and for the effects which they produce upon others. This is clearly a psychic power which we all possess, which we are all constantly exercising; and yet how few of us ever think of it or the serious responsibility which it involves.

Inevitably and without any effort of ours every thought which we allow to rest within our minds must be influencing the minds of others about us. Consider how frightful would be the responsibility if this thought were an impure or an evil one, for we should then be spreading moral contagion among our fellow-men. Remember that hundreds and thousands of people possess within them latent germs of evil—germs which may never blossom and bear fruit unless some force from without plays upon them and starts them into activity. If you should yield yourself to an impure or unholy thought, the vibration which you thus produce may be the very factor which awakens a germ into activity and causes it to begin to grow. Later it may blossom out into thoughts and words and deeds of evil, and these in their turn may injuriously affect thousands of other men even in the far distant future. We see then how awful is the responsibility of a single impure or evil thought. Very much harm is done in this way, and done quite unconsciously; yet there is no doubt whatever that a heavy responsibility lies upon the man who knows that he ought to have purified his mind, but has neglected to do so. If it should ever happen to us, then, to have an impure or evil thought arising within us, let us hasten at once to send out a strong and vivid thought of purity and goodness to follow hard upon the other vibration and so far as may be, undo any evil which it may have done.

Most happily all this is also true of good thought as well

as of evil; and the man who realizes this may set himself to work to be a veritable sun, constantly radiating upon all his neighbors thoughts of love and calm and peace. This is a very grand psychic power, and yet it is one that is within the reach of every human being—of the poorest as well as the wealthiest, of the little child as well as of the great sage. How clearly this consideration shows us the duty of controlling our thought and of keeping it always at the highest level which is possible for us!

That, however, is only one of the results of thought. Our clairvoyant watching the genesis of this thought would see that it not only sets up this radiating and divergent vibration, but that it also makes a definite form. All students of Theosophy are acquainted with the idea of the elemental essence that strange half-intelligent life which surrounds us in all directions; and they know how very readily it responds to the influence of the human thought, and how every impulse sent out from the mind-body of man immediately clothes itself in a temporary vehicle of this essence. Thus it becomes for the time being a kind of living creature, the thought-force being the soul and the elemental essence the body. There may be infinite variety in the color and shape of such thought-forms, or artificial elementals, as they are sometimes called. Each thought draws round it the matter which is appropriate for its expression and sets that matter into vibration in harmony with its own; thus the character of the thought decides its color, and the study of its variations and combinations is an exceedingly interesting one. A list of these colors with their signification is given in the book which I have just mentioned, "Man Visible and Invisible," and a number of colored drawings of various types of thought forms will be found accompanying Mrs. Besant's article on the subject in Lucifer for September, 1896. In very many cases these thoughts are merely revolving clouds of the color appropriate to the special idea which gave them birth; but in the case of a really definite form, a clear cut and often very beautiful shape will be assumed. If the thought be purely intellectual and impersonal—for example if the thinker is attempting to solve a problem in algebra or geometry—then his thought-forms and waves of vibration will be confined to the mental plane. If, however, his thought is of a spiritual nature, or is tinged with love and aspiration or deep unselfish feeling, then it will rise upwards from the mental plane and will borrow much of the splendor and glory of the Buddhic levels above. In such a case its influence is exceedingly powerful, and every such thought is a mighty force for good which cannot but produce decided effect upon all other mental bodies within reach, if they contain any quality at all capable of response. If, on the other hand, the thought has in it something of self or of personal desire, at once its vibrations turn downward, and it draws around itself a body of astral matter in addition to its clothing of mental matter. Thus then is a thought form capable of acting upon not only the minds but the astral bodies of other men—that is to say, capable not only of arousing thoughts within them but also of stirring up their feelings. Here once more we see the terrible responsibility of sending forth a selfish thought or one charged with low and evil magnetism. If any man about us has a weak spot within his nature—and who has not?—then this selfish thought of ours may find that weak spot and develop the germ into poisonous fruit and flower. Once more, purely good and loving thoughts and feelings will project their forms also, and will act upon other men just as strongly in their way as did the evil in the contrary direction; so that this opens before us a sphere of usefulness, when once our thoughts and feelings are thoroughly under the control of the higher self.

THOUGHT FORMS.

It may be useful for us to think a little more closely of this thought-form, and to note its further adventures. Often a man's thought is definitely directed towards some one else— that is to say, he sends forth from himself a thought of affection, of gratitude, or unfortunately it may sometimes be of envy or jealousy or of hatred towards some one else. Such a thought will produce its radiations precisely as would any other; but the thought form which it generates is imbued with the definite intention, as it were, and as soon as it breaks away from the mental and astral bodies of the thinker it goes straight towards the person upon whom it is directed, and fastens itself upon him. It may be compared not inaptly to a Leyden jar, with its charge of electricity. If the man towards whom it is directed is at the moment in a passive condition, or if he has within him active vibrations of a character harmonious with its own, it will at once discharge itself upon him. Its effect will naturally be to provoke a vibration similar to its own if none such already exists, or to intensify it if it is already to be found there. If the man's mind is so strongly occupied along some other lines that it is impossible for the vibration to find an entrance, the thought form hovers about him waiting for an opportunity to discharge itself.

Unfortunately, however, at our present stage of evolution the majority of the thoughts of men are probably self-centered, even when not actively selfish. They are often very heavily tinged by desire, and in such cases they not only descend into and clothe themselves with astral matter, but they also tend to react upon the man who set them in motion. Many a man may be seen surrounded by a shell of thought-forms, all of them hovering closely about him and constantly reacting upon him. The tendency in such a case is naturally to reproduce themselves—that is to say, to stir up in him a repetition of the thoughts to which he has previously yielded himself. Many a man feels this pressure upon him from without—this constant suggestion of certain thoughts; and if the thoughts are evil he frequently thinks of them as tempting demons goading him into sin. Yet they are none the less entirely his own creation, and thus, as ever, man is his own tempter.

Note on the other hand the happiness which this knowledge brings to us and the enormous power which it places in our hands. See how we can utilize this when we know (and who does not?) of some one who is in sorrow or in suffering. We may not be able to do anything for the man on the physical plane; there are often many reasons which prevent the giving of physical help, no matter how much we may desire to do our best. Circumstances often arise in which our physical presence might not be helpful to the man whom we wish to aid; his physical brain may be closed to our suggestions by prejudice or by religious bigotry. But his astral and mental bodies are much more sensitive, much more easily impressible; and it is always open to us to approach these by waves of helpful thought or of affectionate and soothing feeling. Remember that it is absolutely certain that the results must accrue; there is no possibility of failure in such an effort or endeavor to help, even though no obvious consequence may follow on the physical plane. The law of the conservation of energy holds good just as certainly at this level as it does in our terrestrial mechanics, and the energy which you pour forth must reach its goal and must produce its effect.

USE AND ABUSE OF PSYCHIC POWERS.

There can be no question that the image which you wish to put before your friend for his comfort or his help will reach him; whether it will present itself clearly to his mind when it arrives depends upon first of all upon the definiteness of outline which you have been able to give to it, and secondly upon his mental condition at the time. He may be so fully occupied with thoughts of his own trials and sufferings that there is little room for any new idea to insinuate itself; but in that case your thought simply bides its time, and when at last his attention is diverted, or exhaustion forces him to suspend the activity of his own train of thought, assuredly yours will slip in and will do its errand of mercy. Exactly the same thing is true at its different level of the strong feeling of affection and friendliness which you may send out towards a person thus suffering; it may be that at the moment he is too entirely occupied with his own feelings, or perhaps too much excited to receive and accept any suggestion from without, but presently a time comes when the faithful thought-form can penetrate and discharge itself, and then assuredly your sympathy will produce its due result. There are many cases where the best will in the world can do nothing on the physical plane; but there is no conceivable case in which either on the mental or the astral plane some relief cannot be given by steady concentrated loving thought.

The phenomena of mental cure show how powerful thought may be even on the physical plane, and since it acts so much more easily on the astral and the mental we may realize very vividly how tremendous a power is ours if we will but exercise it. Remember always to think of a person as you wish him to be; the image which you thus make of him will naturally act powerfully upon him and tend to draw him gradually into harmony with itself. Fix your thought upon the good qualities of your friends, because in thinking of any quality you tend to strengthen its vibrations and therefore to intensify it. It can never be right to endeavor to dominate the thought and the will of another even though it may be for what seems a good end; but it is always right to hold up before a man a high ideal of himself and to wish very strongly that he may presently be enabled to attain it. In this way your steady train of thought will always act upon those you love; and remember that at the same time it is acting upon yourself also, and you can utilize it to train thought power within yourself, so that it will become ever stronger and more definite.

If you know of certain defects or vices in a man's character, then send to him strong thoughts of the contrary virtues, so that these may by degrees be built into his character. Never under any circumstances dwell upon that which is evil in him, for in that case also your thought would tend to intensify that evil. That is the horrible wickedness of gossip and of scandal, for there we have a number of people fixing their thought upon the evil qualities of another, calling to that evil the attention of others who might perhaps not have observed it; and in this way, if the evil already exists, their folly distinctly acts to increase it, and if as is often the case, it does not exist, they are doing their best to produce it. Assuredly when we reach a more enlightened state of society people will learn to focus their connected thought for good upon others instead of for evil; they will endeavor to realize very strongly the opposite virtue, and then send out waves of thought towards the man who needs their help; they will think of his good points and endeavor by concentrating attention upon them to strengthen him and help him through them; their criticism will be of that happy kind which grasps at a pearl as eagerly as our modern criticism pounces upon an imaginary flaw.

SENSITIVENESS.

There is another psychic quality which all of us possess in some degree, and that is the quality of sensitiveness to impressions. You know that we all receive these impressions at various times. As yet they are only imperfect and by no means always reliable, but nevertheless they may be noted and watched carefully, and used as training towards the development of a more perfect faculty. Many a time they may be useful in telling us where help is needed, where a loving thought or word is required. When we see a person we may sometimes feel radiating from him the influence of deep depression. If you remember the illustration in that recent book of mine of the man who was under the influence of depression you will recollect how entirely he seemed shut in by it, almost as effectively as the miser was shut in by his prison-house of self-centered thought. If you recollect that most impressive picture you will at once see what it is that your thought can do for this man. It can strengthen his vibrations and help him to break these prison bars, to throw off their terrible weight and to release himself from the heavy load that surrounds him. If you have received the impression of depression from him, be sure that there is some reason for it, and that this is an opportunity for you. Since man is in truth a spark of the Divine, there must always be that within him which will respond to your strong, calm loving thought, and so he may be reassured and helped. Try to put before him strongly the feeling that in spite of his personal sorrows and troubles the sun still shines above all, and there is still much for which he ought to be thankful, much that is good and beautiful in the world. Often you will see the change that is produced and this will encourage you to try again, for you will learn that you are utilizing these psychic powers which you possess—first your sensitiveness in discovering what is wrong and then your thought in order to help to put it right.

SENSITIVENESS MISUSED.

Yet this faculty of sensitiveness also may be misused. A case in point would be if we allowed ourselves to be depressed, either by our own sorrows and sufferings, or by coming in contact with depression in others. The man who is specially sensitive will often meet with much that is unpleasant to him, especially if his lot is cast in a great city, or in the midst of what is called modern civilization; yet he should remember that it is emphatically his duty to be happy, and to resist all thoughts of gloom or of despair. He should try his best to imitate on the higher planes the action on the physical plane of the sun, which is so glorious a symbol of the Logos. Just as that pours out its light and life, so should he try to hold a steady, calm, serene center from which the grace and the power from on high may be poured out upon his fellow-man. In this way he may become in very truth a fellow-worker with God, for through him and through his reflection of it this divine grace and strength may reach many whom directly it could not reach. The physical sun floods down its life and light upon us, yet there may easily be caverns or cellars into which that light cannot penetrate directly; but a mirror which is upon the earth and upon the level of the cavern or the cellar may so reflect these glorious rays as that they may reach to the innermost extremity and dispel the gloom and darkness. Just so it sometimes happens that man may make himself into a mirror for the divine glory, and that through him it may manifest to those whose eyes would otherwise remain blind to its glory.

Trouble and sorrow come at times to us all, but we must not selfishly yield ourselves to them, for if we do we shall inevitably endanger others; we shall radiate depression around us and intensify it among our friends. There is always enough sorrow and worry in the world; do not therefore selfishly add to it by mourning over your own share of the trouble and the sorrow, but rather range yourself on the side of God who means man to be happy—set yourself to endeavor to throw off the depression from yourself, so that you may radiate at the least resignation and calmness, even if you cannot yet attain to the height of positive joyousness. Along this line also there is a great and splendid work for everyone of us to do, and it lies close to our hands if we will but raise them to undertake it.

Another way in which it would be possible for us to misuse this qualification of sensitiveness would be to allow ourselves to be so repelled by the undesirable qualities which we sense in men whom we meet, that we should be unable to help them when an opportunity is offered to us. Every good and pure person feels a strong sense of instinctive repulsion from that which is coarse and evil; and from this undoubted fact a good deal of misapprehension has arisen. If you met some one coarse and vulgar you would feel that sense of repulsion; but you must not therefore conclude that every time you feel the sense of repulsion you have necessarily met with that which is terribly evil. If we regard the matter simply from the material level, the reason for the strong repulsion between the man of pure mind and the man whose thoughts and feelings are impure is simply that their vibrations are discordant. Each of them has within his astral body something at least of matter of all the levels of the astral plane; but they have used it very differently. The good and the pure man has persistently developed the finer type of vibrations which work most readily in the higher types of astral matter, whereas the man of impure thought has scarcely utilizedthat part of his astral body at all, and has strengthened and intensified within himself such vibrations as belong especially to the grosser type of matter. Consequently when these two come together their vibrations are utterly inharmonious and produce a strong sense of discord and discomfort. So they instinctively avoid one another, and it is only when the good man has learnt of his duty and his power to help that he feels it incumbent upon him to try, even though it be from a distance, to influence his inharmonious brother.

We have, however, to remember that two persons who are in every way equally good and equally developed may nevertheless be very far from harmonious. Although the difference between them may not be so extreme as that which we have instanced, it may nevertheless be quite sufficient to produce a decided sense of inharmony and therefore of repulsion. It is therefore by no means safe to decide that, when we feel a distaste for the society of a certain person, that person is therefore necessarily wicked. This mistake has so very often been made by good and well-meaning people that it is worth while to emphasize it somewhat strongly. It is true that such a feeling when decided does indicate a degree of inharmony which would make it difficult to help that person along ordinary lines, just as when we feel at first sight a strong attraction to some one, we may take it as a certain indication that here is one to whom we can be useful, one who will readily absorb from us and learn from us. But nevertheless it is also possible for us to overcome this feeling of repulsion, and where there is no one else to give the needed help it of course becomes our duty to do so.

All then should try to realize these psychic powers which they already possess, and realizing them should determine to use them wisely and well. It is true that the responsibility is great, yet let us not shrink from them on that account. If many are unconsciously using these things for evil, then all the more is it necessary that we who are beginning to understand a little should use them consciously and for good. Let us then welcome all such powers gladly, yet never forget to balance them with careful study and with sound common sense. In that way we shall avoid all danger of misusing them; in that way we shall prepare ourselves to use other and greater powers as they come to us in the course of our evolution—to use them always for the furtherance of the great Divine Scheme and for the helping of our fellow-man.

Magic, White and Black.

A Lecture Delivered Before a Chicago Audience by C. W. Leadbeater, the Great Psychic, of London, England.

WHITE AND BLACK MAGIC— ELEMENTALS—NATURE SPIRITS AND ANGELS—EVOCATION—TYPES OF MAGICIANS—TALISMANS — SELFISHNESS OF BLACK MAGIC—ORIENTAL MAGICIANS—SOME SAFEGUARDS AGAINST EVIL.

The dictionary definition of the word Magic is, "The use of supernatural means to produce preternatural results." In Theosophy we cannot agree with that definition, because we hold that nothing is supernatural, and that however unusual or curious any phenomenon may be, it happens in obedience to the laws of nature. We perfectly recognize that as yet man knows very few of these laws, and that consequently many things may happen that he cannot explain; but, reasoning from analogy as well as from direct observation, we feel quite certain that the laws themselves are immutable, and that whenever anything to us inexplicable is produced, the inexplicability is due to our ignorance of the laws and not to any contravention of them. Our knowledge is as yet so very limited in so many ways, that it is not in the least remarkable that we should now and then come into contact with occurrences that we do not understand. We know only one small fraction of our world—just this lowest physical part of it; and even with that our acquaintance is in reality only very partial and superficial. But the average man is profoundly unconscious of the extent of his ignorance; and so he is shocked and surprised at any manifestation which transcends the boundaries of his infinitesimal experience.

With regard to this question of Magic many people will express exactly the same doubt as they do with regard to Telepathy, Mind-Cure, Mesmerism, Apparitions, and Spiritualism; they will say, "Is there any such thing as magic?" There are always to be found those who deny the possibility of anything which is outside their own experience. We have never seen these things," they say, "and consequently we know that all who have seen them are either fools or knaves, either fraudulent or deluded." It is useless to waste argument upon people whose minds are in so undeveloped a condition as that; it is better to leave them undisturbed to wallow in the self-satisfaction of their own invincible ignorance. They are in the position of the African king who was indignant at the shameless falsehood of the traveler who asserted that in other lands water sometimes became solid. Ice was outside of his experience, and so he denied the possibility of its existence; and just at the same mental level are the people who ignorantly ridicule what they do not understand.

If we wish to try to improve the definition given in the dictionary, we may describe magic as the employment of forces as yet not recognized to produce visible results. In very many cases it is the control of such forces by the human will. Once more there are persons who would deny that any forces can be directly controlled by the will, and once more it is simply a question of how much the person happens to know. The inexperienced but conceited man will deny anything and everything; the wiser man who has studied has learnt to be more cautious and so for idle assertion he substitutes inquiry and investigation. The adoption of this latter attitude with regard to the production of physical results by as yet unrecognized forces will very speedily show that there are many undoubted instances of this, and that they may be connected by very easy gradations with phenomena which are quite common and readily accepted.

WHITE AND BLACK MAGIC.

If we accept some such definition of Magic as that suggested above, there arises the further question, what is meant by the adjectives white and black? In this association they are simply synonymous with good and evil. The recognized forces of nature are no more good and evil in themselves than are the recognized forces of electricity, steam, or gunpowder. All of these things may be employed for good or ill according to the mental attitude of the man who employs them. Just as gunpowder may be usefully applied to clear away the rocks which obstruct the channel at the entrance of the harbor, or maliciously used by the evil-disposed person to destroy the house of his enemy, so may the unrecognized magical forces be employed by wicked men for selfish purposes, or by the good man for the helping and shielding of his fellows.

Let us see what some of these unrecognized forces are. Last Sunday when I was speaking to you about mesmerism I mentioned the possession by every man of a certain amount of nerve ether and also of a vital fluid which flowed along with this nerve ether. Both of these, you will remember, can be projected under the direction of the human will; so in that way mesmerism itself may claim to be a modified kind of magic, since in it these unseen forces are manipulated by the human will, and visible results are undoubtedly produced thereby. The condition of the subject may be affected to a very considerable extent; not only may all sorts of delusion be produced, but the limbs may be made rigid and insensible to pain and the man may be thrown into a deep trance. So that we may really claim these two forces of vitality and nerve ether as among those which can be employed and have been employed by Magic.

Another great force which is used perhaps more frequently than any other is that of the Elemental Essence. It will be impossible for me to turn aside from my subject in order to describe fully what Elemental Essence is, since that would require a whole lecture. I can therefore give but the slightest sketch of it now, and refer my hearers to the Theosophical manuals and text books, for fuller information. You will remember that when speaking to you on Reincarnation and on the various bodies of men, I explained how the ego when descending to a new birth drew round himself matter of the various planes, in order that later on he might build vehicles corresponding to each of these levels. It must be remembered that all this matter—like that which the ego draws to himself for his own use, and the great sea of matter which lies outside—is not dead, but instinct with life. This life is essentially divine, for there is no life which is not divine; but it is nevertheless at a very much earlier stage of evolution than the life which manifests in humanity or in the animal and vegetable kingdom. We must then recognize that all this matter is charged with a kind of living essence; and the study of occultism enables us to distinguish between very many varieties of this strange living essence and to learn that the different kinds may be employed for different purposes in magic. The finer and more plastic matter of the astral and mental planes is very readily sensitive to the action of the human will; so that the living force contained in this essence is to a very great extent at the disposal of anyone who learns how to use it.

ELEMENTALS.

Sometimes we read in Theosophical literature of "Elementals." Properly speaking the word applies only to temporary creations built up by the action of the human will out of this living essence and the matter in which it inheres. Such entities are of course only temporary and are in no sense of the word evolving beings. That is to say, the essence of which they are composed has an evolution of its own as essence; but the entity temporarily built out of it has no evolution as an entity, and no power to reincarnate. It may be described indeed as consisting for the time of a body and a soul, for the matter and its living essence makes a vehicle, which is energized by the thought which is thrown out; and the duration of this thought-form as a separate entity will depend entirely upon the strength of the thought force which is its ensouling principle and holds it together. As soon as that force dies away its body of astral or mental matter infused with elemental essence will disintegrate, and the essence and matter will simply return to the surrounding atmosphere from which they were drawn. These thought forms, however, may be exceedingly capable and forceful while they last; and their employment by the will of the thinker is one of the commonest and yet one of the most effective of the acts of magic. An exceedingly useful and illuminative article on the subject of thought forms written by Mrs. Besant will be found in Lucifer for September, 1896. I should strongly recommend it to the careful study of all who are interested in this matter, as the colored illustrations which are there given will help the inquirer to a ready comprehension of the way in which such forces act.

NATURE SPIRITS AND ANGELS.

We have also to consider another class of entities which are very frequently employed in magic; and this time we are dealing with real and evolving beings—not merely with temporary creations. There is a whole kingdom of vivid life which does not belong to our human line of evolution at all, but seems to be running parallel with it, and yet to be utilizing this same world in which we live. This evolution contains all grades of intelligences, from entities at the level in that respect of our animal kingdom, to others who equal or even greatly surpass the highest intellectual power of man. This evolution does not appear normally to descend to the physical plane; its members, at any rate, never take upon themselves dense physical bodies such as ours. The great majority of those with whom we have to deal possess only astral bodies, although certainly some types come down to to the etheric part of the physical plane and clothe themselves with its matter, thus bringing themselves nearer to the limit of ordinary human sight. There are vast hosts of these beings, and an almost infinite number of types and classes and tribes among them. Broadly speaking, we may divide them into two great classes, (A) Nature Spirits or Fairies, and (B) Angels or, as they are called in the East, Devas. This second class begins at a level corresponding to the human but reaches up to heights far beyond any that humanity has as yet touched, so that its connection with magic is naturally of the slightest kind and belongs solely to one of the classes of which we shall speak presently. The Nature Spirits have been called by very many different names at different periods and in various countries. We read of them as Fairies, Elves, Pixies, Kobolds, Sylphs, Gnomes, Salamanders, Undines, Brownies, or "Good People," and traditions of their occasional appearances exist in every country under heaven. They have usually been supposed to be merely the creations of popular superstition, and it is no doubt true that very much has been said of them which would not bear scientific investigation. Nevertheless it is quite true that such an evolution does exist, and that its members occasionally, though rarely, manifest themselves to human vision. Normally they have no connection whatever with humanity or its evolution, and the majority of them rather shun than court the presence of man, since his ill-regulated emotions, passions, and desires are to them a source of much disturbance and acute discomfort. Nevertheless now and then exceptional circumstances have brought some of them into direct contact and even friendship with man.

Naturally they possess powers and methods of their own, and in many cases they can be either induced or compelled to put these powers at the service of the student of occultism. Although they are not as yet individualized, and in that respect correspond rather to the animal kingdom than to humanity, yet their intelligence is in many cases quite equal to that of man. They seem, however, to have usually but little sense of responsibility, and the will is generally somewhat less developed with them than it is with the average man. They can therefore readily be dominated by the exercise of mesmeric powers, and can then be employed in very many ways to carry out the will of the magician. There are very many purposes for which they may be utilized, and so long as the tasks prescribed to them are within their power they will be faithfully and surely executed. All this will no doubt seem strange to many of you, but any student of the occult will confirm what I have said here as to the existence of these beings and the possibility that they can be used in very many ways by one who understands them. I have myself made a considerable study of this subject, and you must therefore pardon me if I appear to speak positively and as a matter of course with regard to many things that for the majority of you would seem questionable or beyond human knowledge. To give a full account of all the many classes of these Nature Spirits would be to write a kind of natural history of the astral plane, and in order to describe them all we should need many large volumes. Yet the man who wishes to deal fully and efficiently with what is called practical magic must not only be able to recognize immediately upon sight all these thousands of varieties but must also know which of them can most suitably be employed for any special piece of work that he may have in hand.

The forces to which I have referred are those most commonly employed in any question of magic; but in addition to them the occult student has at his command enormous reserves of power of various sorts not yet known to the scientific world. There is an etheric pressure, just as there is an atmospheric pressure; but the scientific man will never be able to use this force, or even to demonstrate its existence, until he can invent some substance which shall be impervious to ether, so that he can construct a chamber or vessel out of which ether can be pumped, precisely as the air is withdrawn from the reservoir of an air pump. There are methods known to occult science by which this can be done and so a tremendous etheric pressure can be reined in and utilized. Then there are also mighty electric and magnetic currents, which can be tapped and brought down to the physical plane by him who understands them; and an enormous amount of energy may be liberated by the mere process of transferring matter from one condition to another. So that along different lines there is much energy available in nature for the man who knows how to use it; and all of it is available for and readily controllable by the developed human will. One other point that must not be forgotten is that all around us stand those whom we call the dead—those, that is to say, who have only recently put off their physical bodies and are still hovering close about us in their astral vehicles. They may also be influenced, either mesmerically or by persuasion, just as those still in the flesh could be; and very many cases arise in which we have to take account of their action, and of the extent to which their control of the astral forces can be brought into play.

We may usefully divide the subject of Magic into two great parts, according to the methods which it employs; and we may characterize these respectively as methods of Evocation and Devocation—of command and of entreaty.

EVOCATION.

Let us consider the former first. Although it may act through many different channels, the one great force at the back of all magic of this type is the human will. By this the vitality and the nerve ether can be directed; by this all the varieties of elemental essence may be guided, selected and built into forms either simple or complex according to the work that they have to do. By this perfect magnetic control may be gained over any of the classes of Nature Spirits; by this also the wills of others, whether living or dead, may be so dominated that they become practically but tools in the hands of the magicians. Indeed it is scarcely possible to fix the limits of the power of the human will when properly directed; it is so much more far-reaching than the ordinary man ever supposes, that the results gained by its means appear to him astounding and supernatural. The study of this subject brings one gradually to the realization of what was meant by the remark that if faith were only sufficient it could remove mountains and cast them into the sea; and even this oriental description seems scarcely exaggerated when one examines undoubted and authenticated instances of what has been achieved by this marvelous power.

But in order that this mighty engine of the will may work effectively, the magician must possess the most perfect confidence. This is gained in various ways, according to the type to which the mind of the magician belongs. Broadly speaking, we may classify the magicians under four heads, though of course in a detailed account we should have to take into consideration the various subdivisions and modifications of these.

TYPES OF MAGICIANS.

First there is a type of man who possesses such iron determination and such entire confidence in himself and in his power to dominate nature by the mere force of his spirit that he gains his end by the mere determined insistance upon it. He realizes that his will is the true motive force, and he neither knows nor cares through what intermediary agencies this will may work. He is careless and may even be quite ignorant as to methods; he simply rides down all opposition, as it were, by brute force and does that which he wishes simply through the tremendous force of his unalterable conviction that it can be done and shall be done. Such magicians are very few, but they undoubtedly exist; and if not benevolently inclined they may be exceedingly formidable. They do not need a method by which to gain confidence, they appear to possess it in their very nature.

"The second type of man gains the necessary confidence to command from his very thorough knowledge of the subject with which he is dealing and of the forces which he is employing. He may be called the scientific magician, for he has made a close study of astral and mental physics, he knows all about the different types of elemental essence and the various classes of Nature Spirits, so that in every case he is able to use exactly the most appropriate means to obtain the result which he desires with the least possible exertion or difficulty. His thorough familiarity with his subject makes him feel perfectly at home with it and perfectly capable of dealing with any possible emergencies which may arise. Many such men also make a great study of appropriate times and seasons as well as of appropriate forces; they know exactly at what moment it will be easiest to produce a certain result, and so they gain what they need with the least possible expenditure. This whole question of times and seasons and of periodical influences which wax and wane, is one of extreme interest; but it would take us too far from the main line of our subject if we were to plunge into that this evening; for it would mean the opening up and the review of the whole question of Astrology. It is sufficient for us for the moment if we understand that there are times when, and conditions under which, certain efforts can much more easily be made, so that what can be done only with extreme difficulty, or perhaps even cannot be done at all, at one time, may be managed with comparative ease at another. This naturally implies the existence of influences, planetary or otherwise, which are acting upon and within our world; and the exhaustive knowledge of all this and of their combinations would naturally be necessary for the worker in practical magic.

Another type of magician attains the confidence necessary to insure obedience to his commands by means of faith or devotion. He has so firm a faith in his leader or deity, that he is absolutely certain that any command pronounced in that name must be instantly obeyed. I am not speaking merely of results which may be produced upon the mental and upon the astral planes, but also of quite definite and visible physical effects. You have only to read ecclesiastical history to come across many kinds of exceedingly wonderful cures of physical diseases which have been produced through just such determined efforts of faith as those to which I have referred. The authenticated accounts of the cures at Lourdes in France, and at Knock in Ireland, undoubtedly show that a great many ills, even of purely physical type, will yield before determined faith. Any man who has in this way obtained sufficient confidence will find his will so much strengthened thereby that he will be able to produce the most unexpected results. It should be remembered that it is his own will which brings the satisfactory result—not the intervention of the Greater One whose name he speaks. I know quite well that many most earnest Christians would attribute the healing directly to Christ, in whose name it was performed; but deeper study of the subject will show them that cures precisely similar and quite as astonishing have been performed by equally earnest men in the name of Lord Buddha, or in the name of Krishna, or of any other of the great leaders and teachers of the world. It is the tremendous faith that gives the power; in what or in whom is the faith matters but little. The greater person whose name is invoked may not ever be aware of the circumstances; although if he does know and does in any way interfere we may be sure that it will rather be by the strengthening of the faith and will of his follower than by any special effort of his own power. Yet another class consists of those who believe in the efficacy of certain ceremonies, or of certain formulae. For them and in their hands the formulae or the ceremonies undoubtedly are effective; but in most cases it is not because of any inherent virtue which the forms possess, but because of the entire confidence of the magician that when he employs them the result must inevitably ensue. If you read any account of the working of the medieval alchemists, you will see that they certainly had very many of such ceremonies, and that the majority of them would have considered themselves incapable of obtaining their results without the surroundings to which they were accustomed. They wore robes of certain types, they used certain Kabalistic figures, they waved round their heads swords magnetized for certain purposes; they burnt certain drugs or sprinkled certain essences. Now it is quite true that some of these things have a certain potency of their own, but in the vast majority of cases all that they do is to give perfect confidence to the performer and so to strengthen his will to the requisite point. He has been told by his teachers or his scriptures that all this paraphernalia is effective, and that in using it he will certainly succeed. The man by himself might possibly waver and feel frightened; but with the proper robes and signs and weapons he feels so certain of success that he goes straight through without hesitation.

A magician of any one of these types has at his disposal the forces of three levels—the mental, the astral, and the etheric physical. All of these can be directed by the human will, and in using any one of them a man will undoubtedly set in motion certain vibrations in the others also. The scientific magician will of course choose among these, and so will save himself much exertion. Along the other lines it is probable that the performer nearly always sets in motion very much more force and power, and very much more energy than is at all necessary for the object in hand; nevertheless he also attains his results, though it may be at the expenditure of a great deal of superfluous disturbance and unnecessary fatigue to himself. Without going into details, it is not difficult to see how the man who understands would make choice of his materials. If he were dealing with a man of great intellectual development and keen receptivity on the mental plane, it would obviously be better to approach him on that level by means of definite thought, or through the services of the Nature Spirits abiding there. If, on the other hand, he were dealing with a man whose life was intensely emotional, he would find it probably easier to approach him and to impress him along that line and consequently he would send thought forms veiled in astral matter or would employ the services of the lower type of Nature Spirits whose bodies are built of the matter of that plane. Again if he were dealing with a man of grossly material type, one who had dipped very deeply into the physical plane, it might obviously be better to employ the forces and intelligences which clothe themselves most readily in physical matter. But in all these cases alike the motive power at the back is simply the indomitable will of the operator, through whatever channels he may find it best to work.

We find abundant traces of this magic of command in the ceremonies connected with almost every religion in the world. You may remember that in speaking of Buddhism I drew your attention to a manifestation of it which appears in the Pirit Ceremony; and you will see many signs of it in the accounts given to us of old Egyptian ceremonies. Indeed we have obvious relics of it much nearer to us than that, for you may see them appearing again and again in the ritual of the Christian church. It is well known to all students of practical occultism that of all substances water is one of the most easily influenced. It may very readily be induced to absorb influences of this particular type, and will retain this unimpaired for a long period of time. We see a close analogy to this on the physical plane, for we know that water which has stood uncovered in a bedroom during the night is totally unfit for drinking purposes, because it has eagerly absorbed into itself all the impurities cast off during the night from the physical bodies of the sleepers. It is found that it may equally readily be charged with magnetism of any type, either for good or evil purposes, as will be seen by the accounts of various mesmeric experiments in almost any of the books devoted to that subject. This fact seems to have been perfectly well known to those who established the ceremonies of the early Christian church. Even at the present day upon entering any Roman Catholic church we find at the door a stoup of holy water as it is called; and it will be observed that the faithful as they enter dip their fingers into this water and make with it the sign of the cross upon their foreheads or breasts. If interrogated as to the meaning of this, they will tell us that it is in order to drive away from them evil thoughts or feelings and to purify them for the services in which they are about to take part. The ignorant and boastful Protestant probably regards this as an instance of degrading superstition; but, as usual, that shows only that he knows nothing whatever of the subject. Any student of occultism who will take the trouble to read in the Roman prayer book the office for the making of holy water cannot fail to be struck with the fact that here is undoubtedly a definite magical ceremony. For the purpose of the consecration of holy water the priest is directed to take clean water and clean salt; and he commences operations by a process which is called the exorcising of the salt and the water. For this purpose he has to recite certain forms which, though by courtesy they are called prayers, are in reality adjurations of the strongest type. He adjures the salt and the water successively in the most determined language, commanding that all evil influences shall be driven out from them and that they shall be left perfectly clean and pure; and as he does this he is directed again and again to lay his hand upon the vessels containing the salt and the water. Evidently the whole ceremony is simply a mesmeric one, and the objectionable influence, if there be any, would be very thoroughly driven out by the time the priest had finished his devotions. Then having purified his elements—having removed from them anything that might be objectionable—he proceeds to magnetize them vigorously for a particular and definite purpose. Once more he recites the most determined adjuration and is directed again and again as he uses these powerful words to make over the elements with his hand the sign of the cross, holding strongly in the mind the will to bless. This of course means that he is saturating both the salt and the water with his own magnetic influence specially charged and directed by his will for this certain purpose—that wherever this water shall be sprinkled all evil thought or feeling shall be driven away before it. Then with one final effort he casts the salt into the water in the form of a cross, and the decoction is completed.

Now I have no doubt that there are many priests who simply go through all this ceremonial as the merest matter of form, without putting any thought or strength into it. But I also know that there are many others to whom the ceremony is intensely real—men who do throw very much strength and force into their proceedings; and naturally in their case the water is heavily charged with powerful magnetism and a very decided magnetic result is produced. I myself have very frequently performed this little ceremony as a priest of what was called the Ritualistic Section of the Church of England; and I can certainly testify that in my own case I believed vividly in the efficacy of the operation, and I have no doubt therefore that the water which I magnetized was really effective for the purposes intended. Any one who is physically sensitive may easily tell upon entering a Catholic church and just touching the holy water with the hand, whether or not the priest who consecrated it put real strength and thought into his work.

Consecrated water is employed in many other of the church's ceremonies. In baptism, for example, the water is carefully blessed before the ceremony commences; and even in the services of the Church of England you will still find traces of this, for the priest prays that the water shall be sanctified to the mystical washing away of sin, and as he utters these words it is usual for him to make the sign of the cross in the water which is to be employed. It will be remembered also that churches and burial grounds are especially consecrated or set apart for a holy purpose and there also a special effort is made to scatter good influences so that all who enter shall thereby be brought into a proper and devotional frame of mind. Almost every object utilized in the service of the church was originally consecrated in the same manner; the vessels of the altar, the vestments of the priest, the bells, the incense—all had their special services of blessing. In the case of the bells they were permeated with certain rates of vibration and a certain type of magnetism, the idea being that the thoughts and feelings which these suggested should be spread abroad wherever the sound of the bells traveled—a perfectly scientific idea from the point of view of the higher occult physics. In the same way the incense was especially blessed, in order that this blessing might be showered wherever its perfume penetrated, and that its scent might drive away all evil thoughts or influences from the church in which it is used.

Mesmeric influence is again evident in the ceremony of the ordination of priests; for it will be remembered that not only does the bishop lay his hands upon the head of the candidate, but all the priests who are present also converge their forces upon him and lay their hands upon his head also. Undoubtedly when all present were thoroughly in earnest this would be no mere outward sign but would pass on from one to the other an exceedingly strong influence of devotion and loyalty and would help to confirm within the mind of the newly ordained priest the confidence as to the powers which had been given to him. The student of occultism cannot but see that all these are manifestly survivals from a time when practical magic was thoroughly understood in the church. There is hardly a single ceremony among those used either in the Greek, Roman, or the Anglican churches which has not behind it some true occult significance, though in these days so many people go through them merely as a matter of form and never even think that there may be something real and weighty behind them. In these older days people were not only less skeptical but also less ignorant and those who arranged the ritual of the church knew very well what they were doing.

TALISMANS.

This leads us to consider the question of talismans. There used to be a universal belief that a jewel or almost any object might be charged mesmerically with good or evil influences; and though this idea would in modern days be regarded as a mere superstition, it is nevertheless an undoubted fact that such influence may be stored in a physical object, and may remain there for a very long period of time. A man can undoubtedly pour his influence into such an object, so that this definite rate of vibration will radiate from it precisely as light radiates out from the sun. Naturally the influence put into such an object might be either good or evil, helpful or harmful. In very many cases such magnetic action resembles that of a cordial—that is to say that it is highly stimulant; in other cases it is arranged for the special purpose of calming and soothing the subject so that he may overcome his fears or his agitation. Such a talisman may be magnetized, for example, with the special object of strengthening a man to resist a certain temptation—say that towards sensuality; and there is no doubt whatever that when properly charged it would have a very powerful influence in the direction intended. Here we have at once the philosophy of relics. Every one of us has his especial rates of mental and astral vibration, and any object which has been long in contact with us will be permeated with these rates of vibration, and capable of radiating them in turn, or of communicating them with especial energy to any other person who may wear the object or bring it into close contact with himself. Anything therefore which has been in close contact with some great saint or some especially developed person will bear with it much of his own individual magnetism, and will naturally tend to reproduce in the man or woman who wears it something of the same state of feeling which existed in the man from which it came. I have myself known of many instances in which such a talisman was very effective—in which, for example, it was possible by its means to calm and soothe persons prostrated by nervous disease, so that they were enabled to gain the repose of which they stood in such desperate need. We must never forget also that in very many cases the faith of the wearer in the talisman also comes into play and contributes its quota to the result. If a person is impressively informed by someone in whom he has perfect confidence that a certain talisman will undoubtedly produce a certain result, then his own firm expectation of that result tends very much to bring it about; but nevertheless and quite apart from man's faith in it, it is possible for a talisman to produce an effect even upon those who do not know of its presence. When charged by a really powerful mesmerist certain charms will retain the magnetism for a very long period of time. I have myself seen in the British Museum in London, Gnostic charms which still radiated quite a powerful and perceptible influence, although they must have been magnetized at least 1700 years ago; and some Egyptian Scarabosi are still effective even though they are much older than that. Naturally here also it is possible to charge an object for evil as well as good; and any one who will take the trouble to read Ennemoser's

History of Magic will find various instances quoted therein.

Another side of the subject is that connected with charms or mantrams. These are forms of words by means of which certain occult results are supposed to be achieved. Here also, as in the case of the talisman, definite effects are sometimes undoubtedly produced; and also as with the talisman this result may be produced in either of two ways, or both of them may contribute towards it. In the great majority of cases the formula does nothing beyond strengthening the will of the person who uses it, and impressing upon the mind of the subject the result which it is desired to achieve. The confidence of the operator that his formula must produce its effect, and the belief of the subject that such effect will be produced are frequently quite sufficient for the purpose. I ought, however, to mention that there is a much rarer type of mantram in which the sounds themselves produce a definite effect. Naturally each sound sets up a definite vibration, and an orderly succession of such vibrations following one another according to the predetermined scheme, may be so arranged as to evoke definite feelings or emotions or thoughts within the man. Many of the Sanskrit mantrams used in India are of this nature. It is obvious that in this case the charm would be untranslatable, that it must be employed in the original language and that it must be correctly pronounced by one who understands how it was intended to be sounded. On the other hand it is not in the least necessary for the success of such a mantram that the person who uses it should understand the meaning of the words, or even that the sounds should make intelligible words at all. Instances in which such succession of sounds do not make intelligible words will be found in some of the Gnostic writings.

It must never be forgotten that along whatever line the magician works, by whatever means he obtains his confidence, the forces at his command may be employed for evil or for good according to the intention which lies behind them. We have spoken chiefly of the pleasanter side of the subject, dealing principally with cases in which the will of the operator was employed in order to help; but we must not forget that there have been and are cases of evil will and it is important for us to understand this, because of the fact that such will may often be unconsciously exercised. That, however, belongs to the practical application of the subject to ourselves with which I hope to deal next week when speaking upon the Use and Abuse of Psychic Powers.

INVOCATION.

Let us turn now to the second type of magic, that which works by invocation—that which does not command but persuades. It will at once be seen that this type of magic has at its command fewer resources than the other. Here the suppliant himself does nothing; he simply begs or bribes some one else to do something. The thought form therefore is not at his command nor are the various forms of forces such as etheric pressure or the use of the elemental essence. He confines himself to obtaining the services of definite living entities whether human or nonhuman. Efforts in this direction are made much more commonly than we might at first sight suppose; for you will observe that whenever a man tries to produce a result to obtain anything for himself or to have facts or conditions modified by means of some agency outside of the physical plane, he is in reality using invocatory magic, although no such name may have ever entered his mind. A very great deal of the ordinary kind of prayer for selfish purposes is in reality an example of this. I am of course speaking here only of that lower variety of prayer to which alone the name can properly be applied—that which definitely asks for something. The word prayer is derived from the Sanskrit Prashna, through the Latin Precor and is connected with the German Fragen; so that its original and proper meaning can be only a definite request. Very often people quite incorrectly apply the name of prayer to what is in reality meditation or worship—the contemplation of the highest ideal known to the worshiper and the endeavor to raise his own mind and heart upwards towards that object of worship. But the more ordinary prayer for definite and frequently for physical gains, is certainly an attempt to draw down influences from higher planes to produce visible results, and so comes clearly within our definition of magic. It will frequently happen when two nations are engaged in a war, that each of them will pray for its own success and for the destruction of the opposing armies; and this is certainly an effort to enlist invisible forces upon its side. Fortunately, however, this idea of calling in extraneous influences may be used in a good as well as evil way, and naturally we find that many efforts are made in this way to invoke from above some help for the soul.

Perhaps the most striking instance of this is to be found in the life of the Brahman. The whole of that life is practically one continuous prayer; for to every one of his acts, even the smallest, a special form of petition is assigned. Though very much more elaborate and detailed, it is somewhat on the lines of the form which is given for us in certain Catholic convents, where the novice is instructed to pray every time that he eats that his soul may be nourished with the bread of life; every time that he washes his hands to form the aspiration that his soul also may be kept pure and clean; every time that he enters a church to pray that his whole life may be one long service; every time that he sows a seed, to think of the seed of the word of God which is to be sown in the first place in his own heart and which he in turn is then to sow in the hearts of others; and so on. The life of the Brahman is precisely that life, except that it is on a very much larger scale and is carried into very much greater detail. No one can doubt that he who really and honestly carries out all these directions must be very deeply and constantly affected by it.

We shall observe that although the invocatory magician is much more limited in his field of action that the one who proceeds to command, he has nevertheless the choice of several classes of entities to whom his appeal can be directed. He may beg help, for example, from Angels, from Nature Spirits, or from the dead. We know how frequently and how readily our Roman Catholic friends invoke help from the guardian angels whem they believe to be always about them. That is undoubtedly an effort at invocatory magic, and it may in many cases obtain a definite response; although whether it does so or not, at any rate a result is produced by the confidence of the one who offers the prayer in the efficacy of his supplication. That is the good side of such magic; but it has always a very real and very serious evil side. We shall find that showing itself with painful prominence in the Voodoo or Obeah ceremonies of the negroes. In these the magicians are endeavoring to invoke outside aid in order to work evil upon the physical plane; and it is unquestionable that they sometimes meet with a considerable amount of success in their nefarious efforts. I have myself seen a good deal of this in South America, and am therefore able personally to testify that results are produced along this most undesirable line of activity. The same thing may occasionally be seen in India, more especially among the hill tribes. There it is by no means uncommon to find tribal gods worshiped. And the worship very frequently takes the shape of propitiatory sacrifies, in return for which the tribal deity undoubtedly sometimes produce results upon the physical plane. You will read, for example, of villages in which all goes well so long as the village god receives his accustomed offerings; but the moment that those regular meals are intermitted trouble instantly manifests in some way or other. I myself heard of one case in which spontaneous fires broke out in the various huts of the village as soon as they neglected to look after their tribal deity in the usual way. In such cases there is undoubtedly an entity posing as the deity—an entity who enjoys the worship paid to him or finds real pleasure and profit in the sacrifices which are offered. It will be noticed that such sacrifices are usually of two kinds, either there is a sacrifice of some living creature in which blood is poured out, or else food of some kind, and preferably flesh food, is burnt so that the fumes of it may arise. This distinctly implies that the tribal deity is a very low grade of entity possessing a vehicle upon the etheric portion of the physical plane—a vehicle through which he can absorb these physical fumes and either draw definite nourishment from them or experience pleasure from partaking of them. It may be taken as an absolutely certain rule that every deity under whatever name he may masquerade, who claims blood sacrifices or burnt sacrifices is only a Nature Spirit of an exceedingly low type; for it is only to such an entity that such abominations could by any possibility be pleasing.

It will be remembered that in the earlier days of the Jewish religion horrible holocausts of this nature were frequently offered; but as we come down nearer to the present age and the Jewish race has taken its place in civilization, we find that such sacrifices have naturally been discontinued. It is surely scarcely necessary to insist upon the fact that no developed being of any sort, no angel or deva could for one moment have exacted or consented to receive any form of offering which involved death and suffering. No beneficent deity has ever yet delighted in the foul scent and fumes of blood; and the higher types of religion have consistently avoided such horrors.

SELFISHNESS OF BLACK MAGIC.

The distinguishing characteristic of that evil side of Magic which has usually been called "black" is that its object is entirely selfish. There are many cases in which it is nothing more than this—that is to say in which its object is not to do evil for evil's sake, but simply to obtain for the possessor of the powers whatever he may happen to desire at the moment. Much of the witchcraft of primitive tribes is of this nature, and here also there is no doubt whatever that a certain measure of success frequently attends the efforts of the magician. I have myself seen instances of this, and indeed I once took the trouble to learn quite an elaborate ritual of this nature, which, if put into practice, would have given me the services of an entity which undertook to procure whatever its coadjutor might require. Not only would it furnish him with boundless wealth, but it would also carry out his wishes with regard to either his friends or his enemies. From what I myself saw in connection with other practitioners, I know that these offers could certainly be made good up to very high limits; but the conditions required were such that it would have been quite impossible for any right thinking man to go further into the matter. The ritual required was quite easy of accomplishment, but the agreement with the entity would have had to be cemented with human blood in the first instance, and the creature would afterwards have needed regular food involving the sacrifice of lower forms of life. Much more of such magic exists in many parts of the world than is usually suspected. On the other hand without such horrors as were involved in the type just mentioned, there are many very interesting developments of it.

It is no uncommon thing to find in the East men who have inherited from their fathers the services of some non-human entity, who in consideration of an occasional trifling provision of food will perform small phenomena of various kinds for the person to whom it is especially attached. Usually there are curious restrictions connected with the compact. Almost invariably the human partner in this bond is bound to give to no one the name or description of his unseen coadjutor; and oddly enough in a large number of cases the condition is attached that no money, or not more than a fixed and nominal amount may ever be obtained by the coadjutor's help or accepted for any exhibition of his peculiar powers. I remember, for example, a man possessing such a partner who was brought to me while in the East. In this case the entity attached showed his power principally by bringing to his human partner any objects that might be indicated, in precisely the same way that such things are frequently brought at a Spiritualistic seance. Fortunately, however, one of the stipulations which formed part of their agreement was that the unseen partner should never be asked to bring anything which was not honestly the property of his friend on the physical plane; otherwise a system of wholesale robbery would have been perfectly easy, and it would have been absolutely impossible to trace or punish the thefts. The example of this power which was shown to me was quite conclusive. I went with the magician into a fruiterer's shop and bought a selection of fruit of various kinds, and had it laid aside for me until I should send to fetch it. All that was required was that the magician should see the fruit, so that he might know exactly what there was. Then driving directly home with my magician—of course leaving the fruit behind me in the shop—we asked whether he would be able to produce for us the various items of the purchase in any order that we required. He seemed quite confident of this, and indeed the result showed that his trust in his unseen friend was fully justified. The man belonged distinctly to the lower classes and seemed quite uneducated. He wore no clothing whatever excepting a small loin cloth so that it would be utterly impossible to suppose that he had somehow concealed some fruit about his person. We sat upon a flat roof with nothing but the sky above us, and yet each fruit as we asked for it was instantly thrown down among us as though it had fallen from that sky. In this way the whole of our purchase was duly delivered to us, in the order in which we called for it; and that although we were at a distance of some miles from the shop in which it had undoubtedly been left.

ORIENTAL MAGICIANS.

Very many of the more inexplicable feats of the Indian jugglers are performed under some such arrangement as this. Of course I am perfectly aware that any clever European juggler can entirely deceive the eyes of the average man and can produce results of the most wonderful nature by methods which are entirely inexplicable to the untrained. Nevertheless there are certain definite limits as to what can be done in this direction; and for the production of many of the feats of the occidental conjurer a considerable amount of machinery is required, and often a particular position or arrangement of his audience. The Oriental juggler has to work under exceedingly different conditions. His performances are usually in the open air, even upon the stone pavement of a courtyard and in the midst of an excited crowd which presses closely upon him on every side. It will readily be seen that under circumstances such as those many of the resources of his European competitor would not be available. No doubt most men have heard of the celebrated mango trick in which a tree grows, or appears to grow, from a seed before the eyes of the spectators, and even bears fruit which is handed round and tasted. Then again there is the basket trick in which a child is concealed under the basket and then apparently cut to pieces, though when the basket is raised it is found to be empty and the child comes running in quite unharmed from behind the spectators. And we read how in some cases a rope is thrown up into the air and appears to remain miraculously suspended, the conjuror himself, and usually one of his assistants, climbing up the rope and disappearing into space. Now some of these feats are manifestly impossible; and on inquiring more closely into the matter we find that the phenomena described are produced by means of what is commonly called glamor—a kind of power of wholesale mesmerism without the usual preliminaries of passes or of trance. That this is the way in which some of these tricks are performed I have myself proved by various experiments; so that we need not consider any of these under our present head of invocatory magic—though it is possible that in some cases this power of glamor is exercised not by the conjuror himself, but by the unseen partner who has at his command the various resources of the astral plane. Many tricks on a much smaller scale than the above however, appear to be performed directly by the astral coadjutor. I recollect, for example, a little experiment of which I was a witness, which I think must have belonged to this category. Once more our magician wore almost nothing in the way of clothing, and therefore could not have concealed about him any apparatus by which his marvels could be performed. I was asked to produce a silver coin and to lay it upon the palm of my hand. I held it towards the magician who breathed upon it but did not touch it, and then motioned me back to my seat some fifteen feet away. I was then instructed to cover this coin with my other hand, and as I did so the juggler began to mutter rapidly some incomprehensible words. Instantly I felt the sense of something exceedingly cold swelling between my hands and forcing them apart. In a moment or two this curious cold mass began to stir between my hands, and I opened them to see what was there. To my horror I found that a huge black scorpion had taken the place of the coin. Instinctively I threw him to the ground, and after erecting his tail angrily he scuttled away. Another man present went through exactly the same performance, except that in his case as he opened his hands a small but very active snake was found neatly coiled up between them. Now this was by no means a performance of the same nature as the production of a living rabbit out of one's hat by the ordinary juggler; for in this case the conjurer was some fifteen feet away, and the coin was obviously a coin and nothing else after we had withdrawn far beyond his reach. The result might have been produced by the same power of glamor to which I have previously referred; but certain circumstances connected with it make that to my mind highly improbable, and I suspect it to be a case of genuine substitution by some astral entity.

Another curious little case of the employment of this sort of traditional magic by a man quite uneducated and entirely ignorant of the methods by which it worked, came under my notice some years later. It happened that I had received a somewhat severe wound from which the blood was pouring plentifully. A passing coolie hastily snatched a leaf from a shrub at the roadside, pressed it for a moment to the wound and muttered half a dozen words, and the flow of blood instantly and entirely ceased. Naturally I asked the man how he had done this, but he was quite unable to give any satisfactory reply. All he could say was that this charm which he was forbidden to disclose had been handed down in his family for two generations, and his belief was that there was a spirit of some sort summoned by the charm, who produced the required result. I inquired whether the leaf selected had any part in the success of his experiment, but he answered that any leaf, or a fragment of paper or cloth would have done equally as well. He evidently believed that the effect was wholly due to the form of words employed; and it may have been that it was his own confidence in this which enabled his will to produce the physical result.

In none of the cases which I have described was there anything especially evil or selfish about the magic employed; but I fear that there are very many instances in which the work done in such ways is much less innocent.

Many of the witch stories of medieval times and the curious supposed compacts with the devil were probably examples of the black art on a lower scale. All of this may be paralleled in certain parts of the world at the present day; and the wiseacres who dismiss all accounts of such things as merely superstitious fancy are, as usual, speaking of that which they do not in the least understand. There is, however, no need that any should be nervous with regard to such performances, or should fear that they may be injured in this way by those whose enmity they have incurred. No doubt results are produced, for example, by the Voodoo or Obeah enchantments among the negroes; but it is very rarely indeed that the practitioners are able to affect the incredulous white man. There are cases in which this has been done; but it should be remembered that it can only be done when the evil from without finds something in the victim upon which it can act. The man whose soul is pure and strong cannot be touched by any such machinations. Thus evil thoughts and practices denoted by envy and hatred may work harm among one of two lines. They may either produce fear in the victim and so throw him into a pitiable condition in which disease and evil of many sorts may very readily descend upon him.

SAFEGUARDS.

The man who is perfectly fearless would have a very much greater capability of resisting all such things, precisely as the man who has no fear of contagious disease is very much less likely to be affected by it than the man who is always in terror of it. Any clairvoyant who watches the conditions produced both in the astral body and in the etheric part of the physical vehicle by nervousness and fear will understand quite well why this should be, and will see that the immunity of the fearless man is quite readily explicable on purely scientific grounds. Another and even more deadly way in which such forces may act upon a person for evil is that they may stir up within him vibrations of the same nature as their own. So if the man has within himself the seeds of envy, jealousy, hatred, sensuality, these feelings may be roused to the point of frenzy and he may be induced in that way to commit actions on which in his calmer moments he would look with horror. But purity of thought guards a man entirely from such dangers, and it is therefore quite unnecessary that any man should be nervous with regard to the effects which may be produced upon him by others. A very far more real danger is that we may ourselves unconsciously yield to such undesirable feelings with regard to other people, and so may, without especial intention, be causing evil results for them. That is a much more imminent peril, and one against which we can perfectly guard ourselves only by seeing to it that no thought of malice, or anger, of envy, or of jealousy shall for an instant be allowed to harbor itself within our hearts.

For the rest, the man who is pure and true gives no handle for any evil influences to seize, no door for its entrance into his heart. If his life and his thought be in harmony with the Divine Will, then he may be very certain that no black magician in the world can harm him. Our danger is not in the least that we shall be injured, but far more that by want of control over ourselves, our own thoughts and desires, we may sometimes do harm to others. This practical side of this subject, however, belongs more especially to our topic for next week, "The Use and Abuse of Psychic Powers."

The Rationale of Apparitions.

A Lecture Delivered Before a Chicago Audience by C. W. Leadbeater, the Great Psychic, of London, England.

ABSURD DELUSION—A BIBLE GHOST STORY—VARIOUS MODES OF APPARITIONS—NATURE SPIRITS, PHANTOM BIRDS—CHURCHYARD GHOST—ASTRAL IMPRESSIONS—THE POLTERGEIST — APPARITIONS OF THE LIVING—RETURNING FOR HELP—RETURNING TO GIVE HELP—FAMILY GHOST.

I suppose there are many people who, before discussing the rationale of apparitions, would ask whether it was after all certain that there were really such things as apparitions at all. Not very many years ago few would have thought of asking even so much as that, for they would have dismissed the whole question contemptuously without a second thought. But man has grown a little wiser since then, and public opinion has changed somewhat on these points. I believe that this diffusion of more accurate knowledge on such subjects is largely due to the action of the Theosophical Society. We who are members of that society have been writing and lecturing upon these matters for the last twenty years and more from a common-sense, scientific point of view, and so a certain effect has at length been produced, and the dense ignorance and iron-bound prejudice of the general public on such subjects have been somewhat modified. The work of another society has also done very much to contribute to the enlightenment of the public mind, for the Society for Psychical Research has devoted itself to careful investigation of these and kindred subjects from the scientific side, and has patiently collected a vast mass of authenticated cases and of unimpeachable testimony, so that for any thinking person the question is settled.

Those who still contemptuously deny the existence of apparitions are simply those who are enirely ignorant of the subject, and are foolishly exposing their ignorance by talking about things which they do not understand. There is a book written by Mr. W. T. Stead, the well-known journalist, called Real Ghost Stories, in which he gives to the world a very fine collection of such narratives, all well-authenticated, with the names and addresses of the various people concerned, so that those who will may inquire directly from the men and women who had the experiences related. No one could possibly read this book carefully without discovering that there was very much more to be said for the reality of the apparition than he had ever supposed before. Mr. Stead himself seems to have commenced merely as an investigator, without any preconceived opinions, but his studies have resulted in very definite conviction, as may be seen from the following quotation from his preface:

ABSURD DELUSION.

'Of all the vulgar superstitions of the half-educated, none dies harder than the absurd delusion that there are no such things as ghosts. All the experts, whether spiritual, poetical, or scientific, and all the others, non-experts, who have bestowed any serious attention upon the subject, know that they do exist. There is endless variety of opinion as to what a ghost may be. But as to the fact of its existence, whatever it may be, there is no longer any serious dispute among honest investigators. If any one questions that, let him investigate for himself. In six months, possibly in six weeks, or even in six days, he will find it impossible to deny the reality of the existence of the phenomena popularly entitled ghostly. He may have a hundred ingenious explanations of the origin and nature of the ghost, but as to the ex-

THE RATIONALE OF APPARITIONS.

istence of the entity itself there will no longer be any doubt."

You see, here is a very decided attitude adopted by a man who has investigated, and has taken a great deal of trouble to understand these things; and his opinion is precisely that to which have come all the rest of us who have made a study of such matters. Surely then it ill becomes a man who has taken no trouble to find out the truth to ridicule the result of the hard work of those who have been more deeply interested in these vital questions than he happens to be. We who study Theosophy know very well that such things do occur, and we know also that there is very great confusion in the public mind respecting these phenomena.

Under the vague general heading of ghosts the ordinary man classes many occurrences due in reality to widely different causes. I propose to try to explain to you a few of those different classes, so that if you should ever come into contact with anything of that nature, you may be able to distinguish one type of phenomena from another, and so know how to deal with them. The American race is a psychic one, and therefore it is well within the bounds of possibility that some one or more of this audience may at one time or other have the privilege of seeing what is commonly called a ghost. I use that expression advisedly; first, because I regard such experiences as valuable from the certainty and clear comprehension which they give with regard to the other life; and secondly, because an opportunity to help is always a privilege, and an apparition usually wants help of some kind. In such cases many people are foolishly alarmed; but if you know something of the subject you will rather observe intelligently, and try to understand what it is that you are seeing.

A BIBLE GHOST STORY.

It is strange that there should be so much skepticism as to the possibility that a dead man should show himself. Every Christian, at any rate, is bound by his dogmas to believe that he has a soul, and he often speaks of it, and of the necessity of "saving" it. I suppose he would indignantly repudiate any suggestion that he did not really believe in its existence; yet if we refer to it as so real a thing that it may sometimes be seen apart from his body while he is living, and that it may survive and be seen after his death, he at once accuses us of superstition and of belief in old wives' fables! How he can reconcile such a silly attitude with the plain teaching of his own Bible, we must leave him to explain. The narrative of the raising of the spirit of Samuel by the woman of Endor, for King Saul, makes a very fine ghost story, and of course settles the question of the possibility of apparitions forthwith for all those who hold the inspiration of the scriptures. Then you may remember how it is written that after the death of the Christ "many bodies of the saints which slept arose, and came into the holy city, and were seen of many." They were seen of many, you notice; that seems rather a well-authenticated ghost story! But most people never think what such words in their scriptures really mean or imply; they just drift along without troubling themselves to understand.

Let us take up in order the various classes of phenomena that people commonly call ghostly, and try to comprehend their nature. We shall find that the genuine ghost is only one class out of many, and we may as well consider the others first. Remember that when a man still living in the physical body sees one who has cast aside that vehicle, and is functioning exclusively on the astral plane, one of three things must occur. The physical body can receive only the vibrations from its own plane, and not those of the astral; so that though there are dead men about us all the time, we are usually unconscious of their presence. In order to see them, either we must raise our faculties to their level for the moment, or they must come down to ours. The dead man who wishes to show himself to the living may sometimes take upon himself for the time a garment of physical matter, so that the physical sight of his living friend is capable of perceiving him; or sometimes he is able to act upon his friend as to raise his power of response to a higher level—to increase his sensitiveness for the time. Thus the physical man may for the time be enabled to use his astral faculty to a certain extent, though it is normally dormant, and so he sees what would usually be hidden from him. The third possibility is that of mesmeric action on the part of the dead man; his strong wish to manifest himself may sometimes act upon the mind of his friend, so as to call up a powerful mental image, which the living man will take for an objective reality.

VARIOUS MODES OF APPARITIONS.

In many cases it is not easy to distinguish between these various modes of operation. If an apparition is visible simultaneously to several people, it is most probable that it is a materialization, because it would be very difficult to mesmerize several people at once, and it is not likely that all of them would be equally sensitive; when one man sees an apparition, and others who are present are unable to see it, then it is most probable that the astral senses of that one man are temporarily stimulated, or that a mental impression has been produced upon him by the earnest effort of the dead man. Many people are already very near the point of the opening of astral senses, and it does not need much exertion of force to open this higher sight for a moment; a very little thing will sometimes do it. A strong emotion has been known to heighten the vibrations sufficiently; there have been cases in which such possibilities showed themselves in sickness in persons who had not been aware of them while in health, because then the ordinary physical impressions which usually dominated them were to some extent weakened. But, as I have said, there is not always a dead man in the case at all, for of our seven classes only one is a direct manifestation of him in full consciousness.

NATURE SPIRITS, PHANTOM BIRDS, ETC.

1. You will be aware from what I have said in previous lectures that we have in the world around us other evolutions besides the human and the animal—evolutions which are normally invisible to us, which have no direct connection with our own, though they share with us the earth on which we live. To one of these we have given in Theosophical literature the name of Nature spirits. Many traditions of such creatures remain in the folk-lore of various countries, and they have been called by many names—brownies, pixies, elves, gnomes, sylphs, undines, fairies, good people, and other quaint and suggestive titles. Do not suppose that all of such tradition is mere popular superstition; there is a vast kingdom of nature of which we are commonly quite unconscious, but occasionally some member of it, for reasons of his own, shows himself to some human being; or perhaps a man becomes temporarily capable of the astral or etheric sight which enables him to perceive the nature spirit; and then, not understanding the character of the phenomenon, the man probably says that he has seen a ghost. Sometimes what the Germans call poltergeist manifestations are due to their action; but we will take those in a separate class.

2. Another class consists of phantom birds or animals.

These may really be ghosts, for the animal has an astral body, which survives the death of his physical form, and he inhabits it for a certain time—much shorter, of course, than the human astral life, but still of appreciable length. During their time of astral life domestic pets have frequently shown themselves to those whom they love, or manifested their presence in haunts well-known to them. I have myself clearly seen on several occasions a "dead" pet animal in his astral body, just as I have often seen him in that astral body during his hours of sleep in his earth life. But very frequently animals which enter into stories of apparitions are merely thought forms, or impressions in astral matter. Sometimes also they are simple accessories to a genuine apparition—parts of the scene that his thought calls up. In what is perhaps one of the best ghost stories on record, that told by General Barter to the Society of Psychical Research, a pony was one of the principal features. As, however, the pony was dead at the time, it is not possible to be certain whether he was an accessory produced by the thought of the dead man, or a real ghost on his own account. In the story of the miller on the grey horse, told to Mr. Stead, the animal is evidently nothing but a materialized thought, and not a real ghost; but it is also quite likely that the miller himself is of the same nature. It is impossible to tell all these illustrative stories at length in one lecture; but all of them, and many more, will be found in full in my new book, "The Other Side of Death," in which I have devoted over one hundred and fifty pages to this subject of apparitions and their classification.

THE CHURCHYARD GHOSTS.

3. Another class is what is often called "the churchyard ghost." This is not strictly speaking a ghost at all, for the real man is not there, and what is seen is usually just as truly a corpse as that which is buried below. Such forms are generally not clearly defined, but vague floating columns, more wreaths of mist in semi-human form than anything else. They are composed of the etheric matter which has been part of the physical body during earth-life, but is withdrawn from it at death. That matter is still closely connected with the physical remains, so it floats above the grave in which they are laid. It reproduces in uncertain outline the form of the deceased, and so is sometimes taken for him by the ignorant; but in reality he is usually far away

THE RATIONALE OF APPARITIONS.

with friends whom he loves, and this is nothing but a cast-off garment, having no more consciousness than an old coat.

ASTRAL IMPRESSIONS.

4. Another class consists of what we call astral impressions. Mr. Stead writes thus with regard to it: "This is a type of a numerous family of ghosts of whose existence the phonograph may give us some hint by way of analogy. You speak into the phonograph, and forever after as long as the phonograph is set in action it will reproduce the tone of your voice. You may be dead and gone, but still the phonograph will reproduce your voice while with it every tone will be audible to posterity. So it may be in relation to ghosts. A strong emotion may be able to impress itself upon surrounding objects in such a fashion that at certain times, or under certain favorable conditions, they reproduce the actual image and actions of the person whose ghost is said to haunt."

This is exactly what does happen. Psychometry proves to us that even the tiniest physical object bears with it forever the impress of everything that has occurred in its neighborhood. Normally this impression remains dormant so far as our senses are concerned, and it needs the peculiar power of the psychometer to come into touch with it; but naturally when it is excessively strong, it needs less sensitiveness to become aware of it, and it may even be so much on the surface as to obtrude itself upon the notice of the ordinary and undeveloped man. Wherever tremendous mental disturbance has taken place, wherever overwhelming terror, pain, sorrow, hatred, or indeed any kind of intense passion has been felt, an impression of so very marked a character has been made by the violent astral vibrations that a person with even the faintest glimmer of psychic faculty cannot but be deeply influenced by it. It would need but a slight temporary increase of sensibility to enable almost anyone to visualize the entire scene—to see the event in all its detail apparently taking place before his eyes; and under favorable circumstances the record may even be materialized, so that every one may perceive it by means of his physical senses.

Sometimes such a record will be only a partial reproduction of what really happened; only a sound will remain to testify to the violence of the emotion which originally caused it. You know how many so-called hauntings consist merely of sounds which recur at regular intervals, or at certain hours. Most of these are probably of this nature. Many years ago I myself had a little experience along these lines—a very trifling affair, yet one which illustrates exactly the law which we are considering. Near where I was then living a new road was in process of formation across a stretch of open ground. As yet no houses were erected, but the road was laid out, and the line of curbstones was already in place on each side from end to end. The road was separated from the broad, flat meadows on each side only by a low post-and-rail fence. Naturally everybody who used the road walked along the curbstones, as the rest of the road was still rough. It was entirely unlighted at night, but was often used as a short cut, as the line of the curbstones was not difficult to follow. Presently, however, it acquired a bad reputation, and was supposed to be haunted in some way, but I never heard any particulars. Still, I have seen men waiting at the end before plunging into its gloom, hoping that someone else would come up, so that they might walk down it together.

One still, moonlight night I turned into this road about nine o'clock and walked briskly down it. A thin mist hung over the fields, but I could see with perfect clearness up and down the road, and across the meadows on either side. When about half-way along (the road was about a mile in length) and with nobody in sight either before or behind, I suddenly heard somebody begin running desperately, as if for his life. He was running along the curbstone, for the clear ringing sound of the footsteps was quite different from what it could have been on soft earth. I know no words strong enough to express the sense of mad haste and overwhelming terror which was somehow implied in these sounds. I thought at once "Here is somebody horribly frightened; I wonder what he has seen or imagined." But where was the man? The madly-hastening footsteps came rushing wildly towards me; I stood still on the curbstone while they dashed up to me, under my very feet and away down the road behind me; yet no visible form passed me as I stood there startled and wondering! There was no possibility of any mistake; but for those loud, insistent footsteps, the stillness was absolute; there was no doubt whatever that they had rushed past me, and there was also no doubt that there was no human being there to cause them. There lay the road, stretching away in the clear moonlight in both directions; the open fence by my side could not have concealed a dog from me, far less a man; and yet not a living being was in sight!

THE RATIONALE OF APPARITIONS.

This was before the days of the Theosophical Society, and I had no comprehensible explanation to offer myself. Now, by the light of Theosophical teaching, the whole matter is quite simple. No doubt somebody had been frightened at that spot—badly frightened—and had rushed wildly away in frantic haste to escape towards the friendly gaslights and human company from whatever he saw, or thought he saw; and so great had been the poor man's terror that it had made a deep impression upon surrounding objects. The astral vibrations of this shock of fear had been violent enough to make the phonographic record of which Mr. Stead writes—that which can reproduce itself upon the physical plane; and it had registered the sound of those flying, echoing footsteps on the stone in such a manner that they could be repeated for my benefit.

We are not yet sufficiently versed in the laws governing such phenomena to be able to distinguish why the sound only should have been reproduced, and not the fleeing form, as happened in other similar cases. But hauntings which consist only of sounds seem much more numerous than those which involve actual apparition; so it suggests itself that the much slower vibrations of sound are more easily registered than the very rapid vibrations which would produce an effect upon the eye. There are many stories of this type, obviously due to astral impression. We know how often a haunting is supposed to take place at the scene of a murder, and often the entire occurrence seems to be rehearsed. Such a case is almost always one of astral impression; for although it is conceivable that the murderer, moved by remorse, might haunt the scene of his crime, it is clear that the murdered man would not be in the least likely to do so. Sometimes such manifestations may be traced to the unquiet thought of the criminal, but more frequently to the impression left by the feelings of horror, fear, despair, intense anger and hatred, which are usually connected with such a spot. Many examples will be found in the new book which I have just written, in which also are recorded many instances of our next class—the curious phenomena produced by what is called a poltergeist.

THE POLTERGEIST.

5. This is a kind of parody upon a real haunting, though it is often even more tiresome and destructive than the genuine article. It is generally merely a temporary display or

mischief, though occasionally it lasts for years. Its commonest form is that of stone-throwing, and of the removal and breaking of all kinds of small objects. Such performances always involve partial materialization, at least as far down as etheric matter; but for this part of the subject I must refer you to what I said last week on the subject of Spiritualism, and to the chapter of personal experiences of Spiritualistic phenomena in my book before-mentioned. There may be any one of several different causes at work when such phenomena are produced. Undoubtedly in some cases malice is involved, and the performance is of the nature of a persecution; in others it appears to be intended as a kind of practical joke. It may be the work of a foolish dead man, or it may be due to an imitative and sportive nature-spirit; sometimes its production seems to be unintentional. There are very many cases of it on record, in different countries and at widely separated dates, and examples may be found in any of the books which contain collections of stories of hauntings. John Wesley's account of the occurrences at Epworth Parsonage is one of the best known, though it was a very mild example of this class of haunting; the well-known story of Willington Mill, and that of the Drummer of Tedworth, will at once come to the mind of any student of this hidden side of nature.

APPARITIONS OF THE LIVING.

6. Our sixth class consists of apparitions of the living, and these naturally divide themselves into two sub-classes —(a) cases in which the man himself is really present, and (b) cases in which the apparition is only a thought-form, and the man himself is fully awake elsewhere.

Of the first sub-class we have many well-authenticated instances. One of the most picturesque is that related by Mr. Robert Dale Owen in his "Footfalls on the Boundary of Another World," in which he describes how a man who was shipwrecked fell asleep, and during his sleep appeared on board a barque and wrote on the captain's slate directions for him to steer towards a certain quarter in order that he might rescue the castaways. The captain is naturally very much mystified, but finally decides to adopt the suggestion, and in due course finds and saves the shipwrecked crew, recognizing among them the man whom his mate had seen writing on his slate some hours before. It is usually only under stress of such serious need as this that a man pays an astral

THE RATIONALE OF APPARITIONS.

visit of the nature described, and makes himself visible to physical sight; and it seems to happen most readily when the man is on the point of death, as the principles are then easily separable. The case of Mary Coffe of Rochester is a well-known instance, and there are several others almost identical. In each of this group of stories a mother is dying away from home, and feels that she could pass away with perfect content if only she could see her children once more; in each she falls into a deep sleep or trance, and on awaking declares that now she can die happily, since she has seen them all; in each case the children and their nurse at some distant point see the apparition of the mother at just the same moment, she comes and smiles upon them, and then disappears. Of the first-mentioned of these, Mr. Andrew Lang remarks: "Not many stories have such good evidence in their favor."

In all those cases the living person obviously paid the visit, leaving his body in sleep or trance; but in our second subdivision the man just as obviously does not pay the visit, because he is fully awake and conscious elsewhere at the moment of the apparition. A case in point is that of a man whose duty it was to be at work at six o'clock each morning—a duty which he had fulfilled punctually for many years; but there came a day when he overslept himself, and did not wake until twenty minutes past six. Exactly at that moment he was seen to rush into the shop where his employer was awaiting him; it was noticed by all who saw him that he appeared much excited, but he passed out through a side door without speaking. Twenty minutes later he came in, also very much excited, and explained that it was twenty minutes past six when he wakened, and that he had run all the way from his house (he lived a mile from the place of business). He knew nothing whatever of the previous visit. This is evidently an instance of the materialization of a strong thought-form; the man thought very vividly of his usual post, and earnestly wished that he was there as usual, and in this way he called into existence the form which was seen by all the workmen present as well as by the employer and his daughter. Nor is this the only example; there are hosts of such stories, and there can be no question that such things frequently occur. Mrs. Crowe has collected a number of instances in her book, "The Night Side of Nature."

Something very similar once happened to me—a small

matter, but exactly illustrating the point under consideration. During my occupancy of a country curacy I was once very much weakened by an accident, and so felt entirely unfit for a very heavy Sunday's work. I got through it somehow, though with extreme fatigue, and towards the end of the final service I have no doubt that I may have been thinking longingly of rest when it was over, though I have no distinct recollection of any such thought. At any rate, when I last wended my way to the vestry, I was much startled to find myself already installed there, and occupying the only chair which the little room possessed! The image was habited exactly as I was, in cassock, surplice and stole, all in perfect order; and there it sat looking calmly and steadily at me. This was before my Theosophical days, so I was unprepared with any explanation for such a phenomenon, though I had heard that to see a wraith of oneself foretold death. But I was far too utterly wearied then to think or care about that; I simply walked up to the apparition and sat down upon it, or rather upon its chair, without even offering it any apology. What became of it I know not, for when I rose from that chair ten minutes later it was not to be seen. No results of any kind followed, and I have never seen a similar appearance since. I can conscientiously say that I believe my attention had never swerved from the service which I was conducting; yet I suppose that the strong desire for rest was present all the while at the back of my mind, and in this sub-conscious thought I must have pictured myself as sitting down and resting when the service was over. It is possible, too, that the weakened condition of my physical body may have allowed my inner senses to act more readily, and have given me for the moment just sufficient clairvoyance to enable me to see a strong thought-form.

7. The first subdivision or variety of apparitions of the living which we have just considered—that in which the person concerned was really present—has many points in common with the most frequent form of apparition after death. Just as, among apparitions of the living, the commonest are those of men at the point of death, so among the apparitions of the dead the commonest are those which come directly after their death to announce it to some one whom they love. Of these there are simply scores of examples; and we may take them for our first subdivision of genuine apparitions. A good case is that of the appearance of Captain German Wheatcroft to his wife in England to inform her

THE RATIONALE OF APPARITIONS.

of his death in battle in India. It differs in no way from a hundred others of its class; but it has attained a certain celebrity because through it an inaccuracy in the War Office records and in the dispatches of the Commander-in-Chief was discovered and corrected. Another case which I recollect at the moment was told to us by a Swedish clergyman— a story of a man who died in the snow, and was seen at the time of his death by no less than sixteen persons, who all agreed as to his appearance, and as to certain peculiarities which were found to exist exactly as described by them when the body was afterwards discovered in the snow.

RETURNING TO GIVE HELP.

Another subdivision of our genuine apparitions consists of those who return to help. Some of the dead are still watching closely over certain friends or relations in earth-life, and any manifestations which they make are for the purpose of helping or guarding those friends. One of the most beautiful of such cases is related by the celebrated English clergyman, Dr. John Mason Neale. He states that a man who had recently lost his wife was on a visit with his little children at the country house of a friend. It was a rambling mansion, and in the lower part of it there were long, dark passages in which the children played about with great delight. But presently they came upstairs very gravely, and two of them related that as they were running down one of the passages they were met by their mother, who told them to go back again, and then disappeared. Investigation revealed the fact that if the children had run but a few steps further they would have fallen down a deep uncovered well which yawned full in their path, so that the apparition of their mother had saved them from certain death. I have no doubt that that was simply a case of the manifestation of that wonderful mother-love still keeping a loving watch over her children even from beyond the portals of the grave. Her strong feeling of the urgency of the case no doubt gave her the power to materialize for the occasion—or perhaps merely to impress the children's minds with the idea that they saw and heard her.

Other interesting instances are those in which the dead have returned in order to procure, for those among the living whom they loved, the religious sacraments or consolations which they considered necessary. Two cases of that nature are related by Dr. F. G. Lee in one of his books; in

106   THE RATIONALE OF APPARITIONS.

one of them two little children call a priest to the bedside of their father, describing carefully exactly where he is to be found. The priest, on visiting the dying man, discovers that he is quite alone, and had been regretting that he had no one to send to fetch his spiritual father. The children, whom he at once recognized from the priest's description, had been dead for some time. There are many instances of action by the dead along lines similar to these. A very remarkable case of the continuation after death of philanthropical physical work is recorded by Dr. Minot J. Savage in a recent number of Ainslee's Magazine. He tells us how a Boston preacher made a speciality of work among the very poor, and had many close friends in that class. After his death he still watched over these friends, and constantly gave directions as to their assistance through the widow of his colleague, who seems to have been mediumistic. He tells also of another recent case of an apparition of a dead father to his son, to warn him of approaching death. These things happen quite frequently close about us in the present day, though few but those immediately concerned ever know of them or pay any attention to them.

RETURNING FOR HELP.

Sometimes the dead return, not to give help but to seek it. The need may be real, or it may be merely imaginary—based upon conventional ideas. The dead man, for example, may be greatly troubled because his body is unburied, or (if he happens to be a Catholic) because the requisite number of masses have not been said for the repose of his soul. He may be troubled with regard to debts which he owes, or with regard to debts that are owed to him; he may be troubled because he has left treasure behind him, or because he has not; he may have on his mind some neglect or some crime which he desires to confess, or for which he wishes to make atonement; he may be moved by remorse or revenge. Sometimes the object for which he returns seems to us decidedly trivial, and not worth the trouble which it must cost him; in other cases his motive is clearly sufficient and praiseworthy. All these cases show us how very little the dead man has changed; the different characteristics and peculiarities of disposition of the various people stand out just as vividly after death as before.

Specimens of all these different classes of revenants and of many others I have given in the new book to which I pre-

THE RATIONALE OF APPARITIONS. 107

viously referred, and I cannot do more than just mention one or two of them here. There was an instance of a housekeeper, a most respectable and trusted servant, who had once yielded to a momentary accession of temptation, and stolen some small silver articles belonging to her mistress. After her death this troubled her conscience, and she appeared years afterwards to express her sorrow, and entreat her mistress' pardon. In another case an Irish woman was much worried about a very small debt which she owed to a grocer—the amount, I think, was 92 cents—and found herself unable to rest in peace until she had arranged for its payment. Another very interesting instance, in which the matter was obviously of greater importance, was that of a Catholic priest who had made notes of a confession which was entrusted to him under the seal of sacramental secrecy, and was then killed in an accident before he had the opportunity of destroying those notes as he had intended to do. Such taking of notes of a confession is very rightly strictly forbidden by the church, and so the priest was in great sorrow and anxiety lest these should fall into the hands of some one who would make a bad use of them. He haunted the place in which he had concealed them for eighty years, until some one came to whom he could entrust the delicate mission of recovering and destroying them unread. That is a very good example of the way in which people sometimes suffer through many years for what seems like a small neglect or failure of duty. There are many who are thus earth-bound after death by some passion or longing. Misers frequently suffer in this way, for some of them still have the sense of property very strongly, while others watch with deep compunction the troubles of those dear to them, which might have been alleviated by the money which is now so useless to them in this new life. Then again the man who has committed a crime often haunts its scene; there are very many stories which show that this is so. I remember a good example which is given by Sir Nathaniel Wraxall—the story of a clergyman who finds the vicarage of the new cure into which he is inducted haunted by his predecessor, who (it appears) had murdered two illegitimate children there, and was so filled with remorse that he was unable to rest in his grave, or rather in the other world in which he found himself.

As I remarked before, the poltergeist phenomena are sometimes unintentionally produced by the clumsy action of a dead man; and occasionally this manifestation takes a form differing slightly from the usual one. Such a case was that of Major Moor, in whose house an epidemic of bell-ringing occurred which lasted for fifty-three days, and was never satisfactorily explained. He wrote a pamphlet on the subject, which brought him many similar accounts of mysterious happenings of the same nature. Incredible as it may seem, such tricks are sometimes played intentionally by silly people—people of the same type as those who think it amusing to play an idiotic practical joke on another man in physical life. A person whose development is at that level does not suddenly become a sane or reasonable being because he happens to die, so senseless tricks are played from the astral plane as well as on the physical

FAMILY GHOST.

Again, there is the whole question of the family ghost, who haunts ancestral castles, and often takes upon himself the function of warning his descendants of the approach of death. Such an apparition may be really an earth-bound ancestor, detained usually by his intense pride of race and his deep interest in the fortunes of his family; or he may be merely an astral impression, though in this latter case he could not warn the house of coming events. On the other hand, such warning may be given by an artificial elemental, or thought-form, as I described in my book on The Astral Plane. There are other types of apparitions, of which I have no time to speak to-night; I must refer my hearers for fuller details to my book on the subject, just as I had to do last week with regard to a fuller account of the phenomena of Spiritualism, and of my experiences in connection with them; for each of these subjects is a vast one, far too great to be exhaustively treated in a single evening's lecture.

Before concluding, however, I should like to say a few words more as to the way in which we should meet a denizen of this wider life, if we should ever be so fortunate as to see one. That may easily happen, for many dead men do return. Often such a man needs help, and it is always a privilege to have the opportunity of giving that. We should try to look at such a meeting from the point of view of the dead man, instead of from a selfish one. Realize that he has probably taken much trouble to show himself, and can do so only for a very short time. Do not foolishly fear him on the one hand, nor try to persuade yourself that he is a hallucination

THE RATIONALE OF APPARITIONS.

on the other; receive him as a man and a brother, just as you would if he came to you for help while yet in his physical body; he is none the less your fellow-man because he has for the time put off that garment of flesh. Speak to him kindly, and ask what you can do for him; perhaps he can speak in reply, or if he cannot do that he may at least communicate his wishes by means of raps or signs; at any rate treat him as a friend, and not as a foe or a bugbear. Teach your children to regard such an occurrence as a visit from a dead man as perfectly natural, though rare; thus you will save them much unnecessary terror and give them an opportunity of some day helping some poor soul who sorely needs it, for all of us are brothers, the living and the dead alike, resting ever in the sunshine of the same Divine Love.

- **GOVERNMENT COVER-UPS**
- **SUPPRESSED SCIENCE**
- **ALTERNATIVE HEALTH**
- **UFO'S & THE UNEXPLAINED**

Call Toll Free:
888 909 7474
NEXUS Magazine 2940 E. Colfax #131, Denver, CO

ORDER YOUR FREE ISSUE!!

Pay the bill which follows to continue your subscription or keep the issue with no obligation

---

ORDER FROM YOUR FAVORITE BOOKSELLER OR CALL FOR OUR FREE CATALOG

Of Heaven and Earth: Essays Presented at the First Sitchin Studies Day, edited by Zecharia Sitchin. ISBN 1-885395-17-5 • 164 pages • 5 1/2 x 8 1/2 • trade paper • illustrated • $14.95

God Games: What Do You Do Forever?, by Neil Freer. ISBN 1-885395-39-6 • 312 pages • 6 x 9 • trade paper • $19.95

Space Travelers and the Genesis of the Human Form: Evidence of Intelligent Contact in the Solar System, by Joan d'Arc. ISBN 1-58509-127-8 • 208 pages • 6 x 9 • trade paper • illustrated • $18.95

Humanity's Extraterrestrial Origins: ET Influences on Humankind's Biological and Cultural Evolution, by Dr. Arthur David Horn with Lynette Mallory-Horn. ISBN 3-931652-31-9 • 373 pages • 6 x 9 • trade paper • $17.00

Past Shock: The Origin of Religion and Its Impact on the Human Soul, by Jack Barranger. ISBN 1-885395-08-6 • 126 pages • 6 x 9 • trade paper • illustrated • $12.95

Flying Serpents and Dragons: The Story of Mankind's Reptilian Past, by R.A. Boulay. ISBN 1-885395-38-8 • 276 pages • 6 x 9 • trade paper • illustrated • $19.95

Triumph of the Human Spirit: The Greatest Achievements of the Human Soul and How Its Power Can Change Your Life, by Paul Tice. ISBN 1-885395-57-4 • 295 pages • 6 x 9 • trade paper • illustrated • $19.95

Mysteries Explored: The Search for Human Origins, UFOs, and Religious Beginnings, by Jack Barranger and Paul Tice. ISBN 1-58509-101-4 • 104 pages • 6 x 9 • trade paper • $12.95

Mushrooms and Mankind: The Impact of Mushrooms on Human Consciousness and Religion, by James Arthur. ISBN 1-58509-151-0 • 103 pages • 6 x 9 • trade paper • $12.95

Vril or Vital Magnetism, with an Introduction by Paul Tice. ISBN 1-58509-030-1 • 124 pages • 5 1/2 x 8 1/2 • trade paper • $12.95

The Odic Force: Letters on Od and Magnetism, by Karl von Reichenbach. ISBN 1-58509-001-8 • 192 pages • 6 x 9 • trade paper • $15.95

The New Revelation: The Coming of a New Spiritual Paradigm, by Arthur Conan Doyle. ISBN 1-58509-220-7 • 124 pages • 6 x 9 • trade paper • $12.95

The Astral World: Its Scenes, Dwellers, and Phenomena, by Swami Panchadasi. ISBN 1-58509-071-9 • 104 pages • 6 x 9 • trade paper • $11.95

Reason and Belief: The Impact of Scientific Discovery on Religious and Spiritual Faith, by Sir Oliver Lodge. ISBN 1-58509-226-6 • 180 pages • 6 x 9 • trade paper • $17.95

William Blake: A Biography, by Basil De Selincourt. ISBN 1-58509-225-8 • 384 pages • 6 x 9 • trade paper • $28.95

The Divine Pymander: And Other Writings of Hermes Trismegistus, translated by John D. Chambers. ISBN 1-58509-046-8 • 196 pages • 6 x 9 • trade paper • $16.95

Theosophy and The Secret Doctrine, by Harriet L. Henderson. Includes **H.P. Blavatsky: An Outline of Her Life,** by Herbert Whyte, ISBN 1-58509-075-1 • 132 pages • 6 x 9 • trade paper • $13.95

ORDER FROM YOUR FAVORITE BOOKSELLER OR CALL FOR OUR FREE CATALOG

Babylonian Influence on the Bible and Popular Beliefs: A Comparative Study of Genesis 1.2, by A. Smythe Palmer. ISBN 1-58509-000-X • 124 pages • 6 x 9 • trade paper • $12.95

Biography of Satan: Exposing the Origins of the Devil, by Kersey Graves. ISBN 1-885395-11-6 • 168 pages • 5 1/2 x 8 1/2 • trade paper • $13.95

The Malleus Maleficarum: The Notorious Handbook Once Used to Condemn and Punish "Witches", by Heinrich Kramer and James Sprenger. ISBN 1-58509-098-0 • 332 pages • 6 x 9 • trade paper • $25.95

Crux Ansata: An Indictment of the Roman Catholic Church, by H. G. Wells. ISBN 1-58509-210-X • 160 pages • 6 x 9 • trade paper • $14.95

Emanuel Swedenborg: The Spiritual Columbus, by U.S.E. (William Spear). ISBN 1-58509-096-4 • 208 pages • 6 x 9 • trade paper • $17.95

Dragons and Dragon Lore, by Ernest Ingersoll. ISBN 1-58509-021-2 • 228 pages • 6 x 9 • trade paper • illustrated • $17.95

The Vision of God, by Nicholas of Cusa. ISBN 1-58509-004-2 • 160 pages • 5 x 8 • trade paper • $13.95

The Historical Jesus and the Mythical Christ: Separating Fact From Fiction, by Gerald Massey. ISBN 1-58509-073-5 • 244 pages • 6 x 9 • trade paper • $18.95

Gog and Magog: The Giants in Guildhall; Their Real and Legendary History, with an Account of Other Giants at Home and Abroad, by F.W. Fairholt. ISBN 1-58509-084-0 • 172 pages • 6 x 9 • trade paper • $16.95

The Origin and Evolution of Religion, by Albert Churchward. ISBN 1-58509-078-6 • 504 pages • 6 x 9 • trade paper • $39.95

The Origin of Biblical Traditions, by Albert T. Clay. ISBN 1-58509-065-4 • 220 pages • 5 1/2 x 8 1/2 • trade paper • $17.95

Aryan Sun Myths, by Sarah Elizabeth Titcomb. Introduction by Charles Morris. ISBN 1-58509-069-7 • 192 pages • 6 x 9 • trade paper • $15.95

The Social Record of Christianity, by Joseph McCabe. Includes **The Lies and Fallacies of the Encyclopedia Britannica,** ISBN 1-58509-215-0 • 204 pages • 6 x 9 • trade paper • $17.95

The History of the Christian Religion and Church During the First Three Centuries, by Dr. Augustus Neander. ISBN 1-58509-077-8 • 112 pages • 6 x 9 • trade paper • $12.95

Ancient Symbol Worship: Influence of the Phallic Idea in the Religions of Antiquity, by Hodder M. Westropp and C. Staniland Wake. ISBN 1-58509-048-4 • 120 pages • 6 x 9 • trade paper • illustrated • $12.95

The Gnosis: Or Ancient Wisdom in the Christian Scriptures, by William Kingsland. ISBN 1-58509-047-6 • 232 pages • 6 x 9 • trade paper • $18.95

The Evolution of the Idea of God: An Inquiry into the Origin of Religions, by Grant Allen. ISBN 1-58509-074-3 • 160 pages • 6 x 9 • trade paper • $14.95

Sun Lore of All Ages: A Survey of Solar Mythology, Folklore, Customs, Worship, Festivals, and Superstition, by William Tyler Olcott. ISBN 1-58509-044-1 • 316 pages • 6 x 9 • trade paper • $24.95

Nature Worship: An Account of Phallic Faiths and Practices Ancient and Modern, by the Author of Phallicism with an Introduction by Tedd St. Rain. ISBN 1-58509-049-2 • 112 pages • 6 x 9 • trade paper • illustrated • $12.95

Life and Religion, by Max Muller. ISBN 1-885395-10-8 • 237 pages • 5 1/2 x 8 1/2 • trade paper • $14.95

Jesus: God, Man, or Myth? An Examination of the Evidence, by Herbert Cutner. ISBN 1-58509-072-7 • 304 pages • 6 x 9 • trade paper • $23.95

Pagan and Christian Creeds: Their Origin and Meaning, by Edward Carpenter. ISBN 1-58509-024-7 • 316 pages • 5 1/2 x 8 1/2 • trade paper • $24.95

The Christ Myth: A Study, by Elizabeth Evans. ISBN 1-58509-037-9 • 136 pages • 6 x 9 • trade paper • $13.95

Popery: Foe of the Church and the Republic, by Joseph F. Van Dyke. ISBN 1-58509-058-1 • 336 pages • 6 x 9 • trade paper • illustrated • $25.95

Career of Religious Ideas, by Hudson Tuttle. ISBN 1-58509-066-2 • 172 pages • 5 x 8 • trade paper • $15.95

Buddhist Suttas: Major Scriptural Writings from Early Buddhism, by T.W. Rhys Davids. ISBN 1-58509-079-4 • 376 pages • 6 x 9 • trade paper • $27.95

Early Buddhism, by T. W. Rhys Davids. Includes **Buddhist Ethics: The Way to Salvation?,** by Paul Tice. ISBN 1-58509-076-X • 112 pages • 6 x 9 • trade paper • $12.95

The Fountain-Head of Religion: A Comparative Study of the Principal Religions of the World and a Manifestation of their Common Origin from the Vedas, by Ganga Prasad. ISBN 1-58509-054-9 • 276 pages • 6 x 9 • trade paper • $22.95

India: What Can It Teach Us?, by Max Muller. ISBN 1-58509-064-6 • 284 pages • 5 1/2 x 8 1/2 • trade paper • $22.95

Matrix of Power: How the World has Been Controlled by Powerful People Without Your Knowledge, by Jordan Maxwell. ISBN 1-58509-120-0 • 104 pages • 6 x 9 • trade paper • $12.95

Cyberculture Counterconspiracy: A Steamshovel Web Reader, Volume One, edited by Kenn Thomas. ISBN 1-58509-125-1 • 180 pages • 6 x 9 • trade paper • illustrated • $16.95

Cyberculture Counterconspiracy: A Steamshovel Web Reader, Volume Two, edited by Kenn Thomas. ISBN 1-58509-126-X • 132 pages • 6 x 9 • trade paper • illustrated • $13.95

Oklahoma City Bombing: The Suppressed Truth, by Jon Rappoport. ISBN 1-885395-22-1 • 112 pages • 5 1/2 x 8 1/2 • trade paper • $12.95

The Protocols of the Learned Elders of Zion, by Victor Marsden. ISBN 1-58509-015-8 • 312 pages • 6 x 9 • trade paper • $24.95

Secret Societies and Subversive Movements, by Nesta H. Webster. ISBN 1-58509-092-1 • 432 pages • 6 x 9 • trade paper • $29.95

The Secret Doctrine of the Rosicrucians, by Magus Incognito. ISBN 1-58509-091-3 • 256 pages • 6 x 9 • trade paper • $20.95

The Origin and Evolution of Freemasonry: Connected with the Origin and Evolution of the Human Race, by Albert Churchward. ISBN 1-58509-029-8 • 240 pages • 6 x 9 • trade paper • $18.95

The Lost Key: An Explanation and Application of Masonic Symbols, by Prentiss Tucker. ISBN 1-58509-050-6 • 192 pages • 6 x 9 • trade paper • illustrated • $15.95

The Character, Claims, and Practical Workings of Freemasonry, by Rev. C.G. Finney. ISBN 1-58509-094-8 • 288 pages • 6 x 9 • trade paper • $22.95

The Secret World Government or "The Hidden Hand": The Unrevealed in History, by Maj.-Gen., Count Cherep-Spiridovich. ISBN 1-58509-093-X • 270 pages • 6 x 9 • trade paper • $21.95

The Magus, Book One: A Complete System of Occult Philosophy, by Francis Barrett. ISBN 1-58509-031-X • 200 pages • 6 x 9 • trade paper • illustrated • $16.95

The Magus, Book Two: A Complete System of Occult Philosophy, by Francis Barrett. ISBN 1-58509-032-8 • 220 pages • 6 x 9 • trade paper • illustrated • $17.95

The Magus, Book One and Two: A Complete System of Occult Philosophy, by Francis Barrett. ISBN 1-58509-033-6 • 420 pages • 6 x 9 • trade paper • illustrated • $34.90

The Key of Solomon The King, by S. Liddell MacGregor Mathers. ISBN 1-58509-022-0 • 152 pages • 6 x 9 • trade paper • illustrated • $12.95

Magic and Mystery in Tibet, by Alexandra David-Neel. ISBN 1-58509-097-2 • 352 pages • 6 x 9 • trade paper • $26.95

The Comte de St. Germain, by I. Cooper Oakley. ISBN 1-58509-068-9 • 280 pages • 6 x 9 • trade paper • illustrated • $22.95

Alchemy Rediscovered and Restored, by A. Cockren. ISBN 1-58509-028-X • 156 pages • 5 1/2 x 8 1/2 • trade paper • $13.95

The 6th and 7th Books of Moses, with an Introduction by Paul Tice. ISBN 1-58509-045-X • 188 pages • 6 x 9 • trade paper • illustrated • $16.95

www.ingramcontent.com/pod-product-compliance
Lightning Source LLC
Chambersburg PA
CBHW031650040426
42453CB00006B/255